P9-DWB-724

PRAISE FOR
Designing with Succulents

"It's inspiring, practical, and complete—a treasure for any
gardener who loves these otherworldly beauties."
—KATHLEEN N. BRENZEL, *Sunset* magazine

"One can't help but be inspired by photographs that induce sighs
and daydreams, and not a small amount of garden envy."
—MARIANA GREENE, *Dallas Morning News*

"Baldwin hit the mark with her detailed work. . . . Her easy to
understand writing style is user friendly to the backyard gardener, yet the
breadth of information is just as appealing to the expert. Stellar photographs
and detailed captions connect readers with plants that are little known and
less often understood. . . . Baldwin should be commended for what might
be the best succulent landscaping book written to date."
—MAUREEN GILMER, Scripps Howard News Service

"A solid overview for landscape architects working with succulents."
—*Landscape Architecture*

"The advice given is wise and borne of the author's
firsthand experience, . . . full of great ideas
with illustrations to match."
—NIGEL TAYLOR, *Gardens Illustrated*

Succulent Container Gardens

Design Eye-Catching Displays with 350 Easy-Care Plants

DEBRA LEE BALDWIN

TIMBER PRESS

Portland * London

Frontispiece: Three pots illustrate the design principles of contrast and repetition. The tall pot's texture repeats that of the *Euphorbia flanaganii* it contains; the red pot echoes the color of *Echeveria* 'Perle von Nurnberg'; and the small terracotta pot is round like its sempervivum rosettes, which also present dainty multiples. California Cactus Center nursery, Pasadena, CA.

Page 6: A rolled-rim pot serves as a focal point for a garden vignette planted with opuntia cactus and *Agave attenuata*. Peggy Petitmermet garden, Elfin Forest, CA.

Published in 2010 by Timber Press, Inc.

The Haseltine Building
133 S.W. Second Avenue, Suite 450
Portland, Oregon 97204-3527
www.timberpress.com

2 The Quadrant
135 Salusbury Road
London NW6 6RJ
www.timberpress.co.uk

ISBN-13: 978-0-88192-959-1

Printed in China

Library of Congress Cataloging-in-Publication Data

Baldwin, Debra Lee.
  Succulent container gardens : design eye-catching displays with 350 easy-care plants / Debra Lee Baldwin. — 1st ed.
     p. cm.
  Includes bibliographical references and index.
  ISBN 978-0-88192-959-1
  1. Succulent plants. 2. Container gardening. I. Title.
  SB438.B257 2010
  635.9'525—dc22   2009016606

A catalog record for this book is also available from the British Library.

TO JAMES

CONTENTS

ACKNOWLEDGMENTS

I am grateful to horticulturists and nursery owners who gave significant amounts of time to proofread part or all of the manuscript: Michael and Joyce Buckner of The Plant Man nursery, San Diego; Patrick Anderson; Dave Bernstein of Cactus Ranch nursery, Reseda, CA; Jeff Moore of Solana Succulents nursery, Solana Beach, CA; and Nick Wilkinson of Grow nursery, Cambria, CA.

Succulent experts Rosemarie Armstrong, Alan Beverly, Tom Glavich, Kelly Griffin, Steven Hammer, Jeff Harris, Panayoti Kelaidis, Bob Kent, Woody Minnich, and Ray Stephenson graciously shared their specialized knowledge. For contributing photos that enriched the text, my gratitude goes to Terri Collins of Washington; Davis Dalbok of Living Green, San Francisco; Iseli Nursery in Oregon; Mari and Andrew Malcolm of Seattle; Frank Mitzel of San Diego; Robin Lee Reed of Ohio; and Nick Wilkinson.

Designers, nursery owners, artists, and collectors whose creativity enhances these pages include Ken and Deena Altman, Altman Plants; Barbara Baker; Art and Sandra Baldwin; Randy and Heide Baldwin, San Marcos Growers; Barrels & Branches nursery; Gary Bartl; Sydney Baumgartner; Debi Beard; Jim Bishop; John Bleck; Charlene Bonney; Karla Bonoff; Brandon Bullard, Desert Theater; Mujiba Cabugos; Cambria Nursery and Florist; Louisa Campagna; Bette Childs; Anna Clark; Beverly and R. C. "the King of Succulents" Cohen; Mike Cone; Diane Dunhill; Linda Estrin; EuroAmerican Propagators; Phil Favell; David Feix; Mary Friestedt; Stephen Gabor; Scott Glenn; Anna Goeser and Pot-ted; Larry Grammer and the Thongthiraj sisters of California Cactus Center nursery; Whitney Green; Erik Gronborg; Flora Grubb and Kevin Smith of Flora Grubb Gardens nursery; Karen Haataja, Timberline Gardens nursery; Tita Heimpel, Courtyard Pottery; Buck Hemenway; Thomas Hobbs, Southlands nursery; Hap Hollibaugh, Cactus Jungle nursery; Jerry Hunter and Heather Hunter May, Rancho Soledad nursery; Evelyn Jacob and Mindy Rosenblatt; Tom Jesch, Daylily Hill nursery; Dan Johnson; Kara nursery; Sandy Koepke; Tony Krock and Margarita Huerta, Terra Sol Garden Center; Marilee Kuhlmann; Kathy LaFleur; Rob Lane; Heather Lenkin; Fran and Clint Levin; Rudy Lime; Sylvia Lin; Matthew Maggio; Wanda Mallen; Bonnie Manion; Sam Maybery, Seaside

Aloe variegata (partridge breast aloe) is beautiful but sensitive to overwatering. Gelfand-Misch garden, Santa Monica, CA. Design by Marilee Kuhlmann, Comfort Zones Garden Design, Los Angeles, CA.

Gardens nursery; Mia McCarville, Cedros Gardens nursery; Pat McWhinney; Monty Montgomery; Laura Morton; Felix Navarro, The Juicy Leaf; Leo O'Brian, Irvine Community Development Company; Peggy Petitmermet; Jolee Pink; Cleo Pirtle, Grewsome Gardens nursery; Ellen Spector Platt; Jim and Sally Prine; Margee Rader; Christi and Richard Reed; Sergio Regalado, Plantplay nursery; the Plum Beach Garden Club of Rhode Island; Al Richter; Mary Rodriguez; Roger's Gardens nursery; Suzy Schaefer; Carolyn Schaer; Schnetz Landscape; Eric Schrader, Bonsai Society of San Francisco; Bruce Shanks, Cottage Gardens of Petaluma & Bennett Valley; Joe Stead, Orange Coast College; Robin Stockwell, Succulent Gardens; Susan and Melissa Teisl and Leah Winetz, Chicweed; Tropic World nursery; Julie Vanderwilt; Howard Vieweg, Sunshine Gardens nursery; Vivai Piante Schiavo nursery; Pamela Volante; Peter Walkowiak; Molly Wood; Lynn Woodbury; Don and Jill Young; and Liz Youngflesh, Garden Glories nursery.

Many thanks, as well, to these public gardens: Chanticleer Garden, Wayne, PA; Denver Botanic Garden; The Living Desert, Palm Desert, CA; Lotusland, Santa Barbara, CA; Ruth Bancroft Garden, Walnut Creek, CA; Sherman Gardens, Corona Del Mar, CA; Quail Botanical Gardens, Encinitas, CA; University of California Botanical Garden, Berkeley; the Water Conservation Garden at Cuyamaca College, El Cajon, CA; and West Green House Gardens, Hampshire, England.

For their editorial professionalism and dedication to quality, I am grateful to Eve Goodman at Timber Press and to Lorraine Anderson. I also acknowledge my husband, Jeff Walz, for kindnesses too extensive to enumerate (including limitless patience); and for his expertise in all things digital and electronic, without which this book would not be possible.

PREFACE

Whether on a sunny windowsill or in a greenhouse, on a patio or beneath a skylight, container-grown succulents offer all the pleasures of in-ground gardening at a more relaxed pace. These are plants that allow you to be lazy. If you are time stressed, are frequently away from home, or have limited mobility, succulents enable you to garden on your own terms.

A succulent is any plant that stores water in juicy tissues in order to survive drought. Because most come from regions of the world with harsh growing conditions, succulents need trimming, repotting, watering, and fertilizing less often than typical container-grown plants.

Initially, I changed my windowsill pots and those in my outdoor living spaces to succulents because I had become captivated by their geometric beauty. I quickly gained an appreciation for the convenience and correctness of owning these camels of the plant world. I no longer ask a neighbor to tend my potted plants when I am away, because they easily survive several weeks without me. If overwatered, succulents may succumb to rot (this is especially true of cacti), but overall, I have found no other plants to be as trouble free.

Every succulent has personality. Echeverias come in sunrise hues and have fat, frilly foliage. Leaves of pachyphytums are opalescent and shaped like grapes. Small succulents—graptopetalums, sempervivums, and the like—resemble stars, roses, and daisies. And few plants can match the edgy yet elegant qualities of a toothed agave or spiny opuntia.

Readers of my earlier book, *Designing with Succulents*, have shown me that people everywhere are eager to grow these easy-care plants. But many beautiful succulents—such as kalanchoes from Madagascar, aeoniums from the Canary Islands, and haworthias from South Africa—are frost tender and thrive outdoors year-round only in USDA zones 9 and 10. Container culture offers an ideal solution; anyone, anywhere can grow succulents in pots, which can be sheltered indoors.

Containers not only protect jewel-like cacti and succulents from the rigors of the open garden, they also allow you better control over the soil, moisture, light, and warmth your plants receive. And should you move, pots let you take your horticultural treasures with you.

Because of their durability, variety, and strongly defined shapes, succulents offer the potential for design that is imaginative and out of the ordinary.

They are sculptural, so your compositions likely will succeed aesthetically even if using succulents is new to you. And when you garden within containers, you risk relatively little in terms of time and materials.

In addition to helping people worldwide cultivate and enjoy succulents, this sequel introduces exceptional kinds once considered rare. To meet a growing demand, nurseries and garden centers now offer a greater selection, and the online marketplace has expanded as well. This book, like the previous one, presents succulent gardens by innovative designers in the United States and beyond. The creations of these florists, nurserymen, landscapers, plant collectors, and home gardeners are eye catching and intriguing—and chosen to inspire you.

Part One offers design criteria you can use to enhance your own arrangements and enjoy those made by others, and describes how to create simple, effective, eye-catching combinations. You will also find guidance on selecting containers that range from pots at garden centers to antiques and flea-market finds.

Part Two presents a specialized palette of succulents well suited to container culture—approximately 100 genera, 275 species, and 90 varieties—plus companion plants. In addition to design ideas in the descriptions, photos illustrate numerous ways to showcase the plants in pots.

Part Three delves into the unexpected—how designers use succulents in intriguing ways. You will find suggestions for many areas of your home, including patio groupings, wreaths, and vertical gardens. Imaginative table-top designs include floral-style arrangements, topiaries, and miniature landscapes—all of which make great gifts. Here, too, are bonsai and award-winning compositions from cactus and succulent shows.

Part Four explains how to establish container-grown succulents and keep them healthy. Included is information on watering, feeding, and overwintering; how to recognize and eliminate pests; and potting mixes. You will also learn how to take cuttings and start seeds, enabling you to produce an ongoing and abundant supply of plants—which will inspire you to create additional low-maintenance and lovely succulent container gardens.

A pot with a fluted rim complements the rippled surface of a bizarre yet beautiful grafted and crested *Euphorbia lactea* 'Variegata'. Chicweed, Solana Beach, CA. Design by Susan and Melissa Teisl and Leah Winetz.

Part One

PAIRING PLANTS WITH POTS

A blue pot is the color complement of *Euphorbia tirucalli* 'Sticks on Fire'. Barrels & Branches nursery, Encinitas, CA.

A well-designed succulent container garden is a three-dimensional work of art. You are the artist, and your palette consists of appealing, fleshy-leaved plants. The container you choose serves as both canvas and frame.

Creating potted gardens is a form of play, and the beauty of succulents can be depended on to redeem less-than-perfect attempts. Apply the design principles of contrast and repetition—and effectively use color, texture, patterns, and lines—and the results will transcend the ordinary and delightfully illustrate your individual style.

There seems no limit to the containers that might be used to showcase succulents. I have seen echeverias growing in heirloom china and agaves lending elegance to corrugated metal pipe salvaged from construction sites. One designer scours thrift stores for interesting objects—from toys to toolboxes—which she plants with cuttings and sells at home-and-garden shows. On the high end are vintage pots with retro styling, and one-of-a-kinds made by artists.

Thanks to their dynamic shapes, succulents look good in almost anything, so as you apply the guidelines that follow, feel free to experiment and have fun.

DESIGN BASICS

Whenever you see a pleasing succulent container garden, ask yourself what about it appeals to you. Go beyond viewing it as a whole and pay attention to its parts—how they illustrate one or more aspects of good design. Notice repetitions, how textures or colors contrast, any dynamic lines, and how well the plants and container suit each other and the setting.

Also notice negative space. This relieves the eye and emphasizes the focal point (a dramatic element that first captures attention, and from which the rest of the design flows). Space is not bare dirt—which seldom looks good, in gardens large or small—but rather an uncluttered backdrop that makes your arrangement stand out, or a topdressing that fills gaps and pulls together the composition.

Contrast and repetition

Contrast and repetition are the two most important design elements. When these are used effectively, the results are remarkable. Contrast jolts and engages; repetition comforts and soothes. One agave in a pot is fine, but repeat that composition—same type of agave, same type of pot—and even casual observers are intrigued and entertained.

Repetition hearkens back to our preschool years, when we were given an assortment of items to group, like with like. Even as adults, we feel a sense of satisfaction in identifying items that are similar and enjoy discovering them in our environment. Repetitions of form, color, line, and texture are as appealing as a new box of crayons, a multicolored set of building blocks,

A wall display of *Agave americana* in identical containers illustrates how dramatic repetition can be.
The Gardens of Appeltern, Holland. Photo by Rob Cardillo.

Even plastic nursery pots look good when contrast and repetition apply. Roger's Gardens nursery, Corona del Mar, CA.

Imagine this composition with *Aloe brevifolia* that has solid-colored leaves rather than variegated. Would you find it more or less appealing? If you like this aloe's striped leaves, the reason is repetition: the pot's ribbed surface echoes the stripes in the foliage. The color of the pot also repeats the leaf color, and the smooth, rounded texture of the glazed pot contrasts with the leaves' prickly edges. Chicweed, Solana Beach, CA. Design by Susan and Melissa Teisl and Leah Winetz.

Red-blooming *Kalanchoe blossfeldiana* (supermarket kalanchoe) is in a pot atop a table of the same hue. The plant's green leaves and square container contrast with the round, red table. Chicweed.

In a circular pot, rounded stones echo the spherical forms of *Euphorbia suzannae*. Al Richter garden, Glendora, CA.

or a series of stepping-stones. But repetition need not be obvious. When it is subtle it is effective, because it engages the subconscious.

What attracts many people to succulents initially is how the plants themselves beautifully illustrate, in their geometric forms, pleasing repetitions. Consider the overlapping, daisylike petals of aeoniums, and the multiple triangles of small agaves and aloes. And when you create containers comprised primarily of succulents, even if the plants are diverse, you employ repetition. Because all have fleshy leaves, whether crassula, euphorbia, or kalanchoe, all say "succulent" to the viewer.

Contrast can be as simple as a green plant in a red pot, but the composition does not become art until repetition enters in: the plant has a slight amount of red in it, or the pot a little green. Contrast and repetition are not limited to color. Appealing designs often have repeating and contrasting shapes, textures, and lines. Examples include a rosette (made of leaves radiating from a central crown) succulent in a round container, a bristly cactus in a glossy pot, a chunky topdressing surrounding a smooth aloe, or a piecrust-rim pot for an echeveria with wavy leaves.

Evaluate a succulent for its defining characteristics—color, form, and texture—and then keep them in mind as you shop for a pot. This works the other way around, too: when you find a container you like, consider which aspect of it might be repeated in your choice of plants. For example, a blue-green pot for *Aloe brevifolia* would repeat the aloe's coloration; an orange-red one would contrast with it. Anticipate a plant's flowers, too. *Aloe brevifolia* has orange blooms, so an orange pot will repeat that color (but only for one month of the year).

If you are uncertain and cannot decide, or want to make a safe choice, go with terracotta. Its soft orange or putty color beautifully contrasts with green or blue succulents. Terracotta combines well with pots that make a bolder statement but is not so muted that it disappears against a backdrop of earth or foliage.

An appealing way to use repetition is to echo a pattern found in the plant with the shape or design of its pot. For example, pair containers patterned with cross-hatching, triangles, or a grid with succulents with pointed tips— such as *Aeonium* 'Kiwi', *Echeveria agavoides*, or *Sempervivum tectorum*.

Ferocactus glaucescens repeats the shape of the terracotta bowl and the top-dressing of river rock, while the plants' spines lend a textural contrast and echo the color of the container. Jim and Sally Prine garden, Santa Barbara, CA. Design by Diane Dunhill.

Repetition need not be complex. Here, four itty-bitty specimens of *Opuntia microdasys* 'Monstrosus' appear to sashay down an oblong pot. A topdressing of black gravel repeats the pot's matte glaze. Adding sparkle are bits of blue tumbled glass. Pot-ted, Los Angeles, CA. Design by Anna Goeser.

The pot's square pattern calls attention to the geometry of *Echeveria subsessilis* leaves, and the blue in the pattern echoes that of the plants. A fine-textured sedum offers contrast. Heather Lenkin garden, Pasadena, CA. Pot by Mike Cone, Phoenix, AZ.

In a handmade pot with lines that repeat the ribbing of the plants, a cluster of *Parodia scopa* suggests an ice-cream sundae. The topdressing mirrors the brown in the pot and in the buds. California Cactus Center nursery, Pasadena, CA. Design by Larry Grammer. Pot by Mike Cone.

White cross-hatching in the pot's design repeats the overlapping, triangular leaves and white lines of *Sempervivum arachnoideum* (cobweb houseleek). Even the plant's rosy blooms match its container. Seaside Gardens, Carpinteria, CA.

The orange of the pot is the color-wheel complement of the blue of both the agave and the senecio.

Color

Leaves of succulents come in every hue, including blue and near-black, so your color palette is extensive. Here again, contrast and repetition will help you make aesthetically pleasing choices. For example, you might repeat the hues of *Echeveria subrigida*, which has teal leaves edged in red, with a teal- or red-glazed container.

Color contrast happens when complementary hues—those from opposite sides of the color wheel— are juxtaposed: red and green, blue and orange, yellow and purple. This translates to a red-leaved echeveria with a chartreuse aeonium; blue *Senecio serpens* with orange *Euphorbia tirucalli* 'Sticks on Fire'; yellow *Crassula ovata* 'Hummel's Sunset' (sunset jade) with deep magenta-purple *Aeonium arboreum* 'Zwartkop'—to name a few.

White stands out in a garden, and black attracts the least attention. *Aeonium* 'Sunburst', which is striped green-and-cream, has definition even when placed against green foliage. But dark-leaved *Aeonium arboreum* 'Zwartkop' looks like a dark hole unless positioned against a light backdrop, such as the sky or a wall. White pots and variegated (cream- or white-striped) succulents, when situated near the entrance to a path or alongside steps, will define the area and glow by moonlight.

A florist-designed gift bouquet of haworthias, accented by gray *Tillandsia bergerii*, illustrates the effectiveness of combining shades of green. Chicweed.

In my succulent sitting area, I painted the tabletop yellow and green to echo the lines of *Agave americana* 'Marginata' in the succulent tapestry nearby. A red pot on the table contrasts with it, repeats the red of pots found elsewhere in the garden, and contains an agave that duplicates, in miniature, the larger one. Escondido, CA.

A topdressing of peach crushed rock contrasts with teal graptoverias in a blue-glazed pot. Inter-City Cactus and Succulent Show, Los Angeles County Arboretum, Arcadia, CA. Design by Glenn and Linda Carlzen.

A cactus (*Opuntia pycnantha*) with paddles that resemble mouse ears has long, golden spines and an all-over bristly texture that repeat in the pot's pattern and color. A topdressing of black pebbles adds contrast. California Cactus Center nursery. Design by Larry Grammer. Pot by Mike Cone.

White patio furniture and pots may be too glaring, especially if there is no white elsewhere—such as a picket fence—for repetition. To tone down white irrigation risers too prominent in my garden, I spray painted them khaki colors. I also have a dog who is white, and not just any dog, but a terrier with crisply pointed ears and tail. White dogs contrast with a garden's browns and greens; black dogs do not, which is significant when you need a companion who is also a photo prop.

Red is the next loudest color, which may or may not be what you want. If you plant red ivy geraniums so that they intertwine with blue senecio and agaves, when you glance at the composition, dots of red will pop and the other plants will seem muted in comparison. In a container in which you thought the main element would be a sculptural agave, a filler plant may instead take center stage.

Close to red on the color wheel is orange, which can be blinding. But when toned down, orange becomes salmon or peach, good hues for lending contrast without dominating. Yellow, purple, and blue when pastel also are gentle. The most soothing groupings of succulents repeat and contrast shades of green. These may vary in intensity and have gray, yellow, or blue tones.

Texture

Texture tends to have a subtle, subliminal effect. An example is juxtaposing spiky plants with smooth ones, such as cacti with agaves. Yet texture also is relative. Viciously spined opuntias, when viewed from a distance, look as nubby as teddy bears. Agaves, yuccas, and furcraeas that appear smooth and sleek up close may suggest sharp swords when seen from afar.

Scale and proportion

Whether you are landscaping a half acre or tucking cuttings into a teacup, scale and proportion are essential for aesthetic success. To be pleasing to the eye, a pot needs to fit the space it fills and contain succulents that are neither too large nor too small. A trough, for example, might have rosette succulents in a row and be used as the centerpiece for a rectangular table.

Turquoise pots hold echeverias, blue senecio, artemisia, and the ornamental grass blue fescue. Golden barrels (*Echinocactus grusonii*) repeat throughout and offer texture and color contrast. Denver Botanic Gardens. Design by Dan Johnson.

A mistake beginners sometimes make is buying an assortment of succulents in 2- or 4-inch pots, then placing the plants in an overly large container; they look oddly small for the expanse they occupy. Using larger succulents

Tiny echeveria rosettes are in scale with themselves and with their diminutive container. Chicweed.

Large pots planted with sansevierias and *Sedum burrito* soften an expanse of hardscape and are in scale with a high-ceilinged loggia. Burnham residence, San Diego, CA. Design by Nick Armitage, Schnetz Landscape, Escondido, CA. Photo by Hewitt-Garrison.

is one remedy, as is applying repetition and contrast. If the plants are alike, spacing them equidistant from each other—perhaps with a topdressing that lends color and/or textural contrast—would be pleasing to the eye.

It may seem obvious that a tiny haworthia does not belong in a large pot, just as a large agave does not belong in a small one. Yet it is tempting to put small succulents that have the potential to get quite big, in large pots, because they will grow to fit the container. But roots of small plants in overly large containers may rot, and aesthetically the fit (scale and proportion) is wrong. Instead, put that plant or cutting—though the offspring of a behemoth—in a small pot that frames it perfectly. It will grow slowly, allowing plenty of time for you to appreciate having a miniature version, precise in every detail, of its parent. A year later you can repot it—or not.

Lines that direct the eye

Invariably, lines will be present that will influence your composition. Think of them as arrows directing the viewer's eye toward or away from the focal point. For example, walkways that intersect at a large pot give the container a position of prominence. Other lines may not be so obvious. A broom handle leaning against a wall will draw the eye away from the container below it, especially if the handle is a bright color. Garden hoses are great offenders; they are ubiquitous and too often a vivid aqua green. Hoses that are black are less likely to shout, "Look at me!"

The pot repeats not only the colors of *Agave desmetiana* 'Variegata' but also its lines. Barrels & Branches nursery.

Lines in this composition lead the eye to the focal point: *Echeveria runyonii* 'Topsy Turvy'. Lunenfeld garden, West Hollywood, CA. Design by Laura Morton, Los Angeles, CA.

Large succulents—such as agaves, yuccas, dasylirions, and furcraeas—that have boldly dynamic lines look good against a wall, the sky, or a blur of foliage. Ornamental grasses as companion plants also utilize lines, yet the effect is softer and is enhanced by wind-generated motion. Contrast might enter in with hard surfaces and circles, such as a curved wall, a round table, or spherical containers.

The lines of a glass-topped table's wrought-iron base call attention to an arrangement of echeverias and sedums. Barbara Baker residence, Rancho Santa Fe, CA. Design by Chicweed.

Columnar *Pilosocereus pachycladus* contrasts with the pool's curved lines and with those of its container. Scott Glenn garden, Santa Barbara, CA.

Architectural lines zero in on a pedestal pot planted with *Sedum rubrotinctum* 'Pork and Beans'. Ken and Deena Altman residence, Escondido, CA.

Lines also can detract—and distract—from a composition. Allow pine needles to fall into your container arrangement, for example, and it will be marred by lines as unappealing as scratches on a painting.

AT THE NURSERY

The easiest way to pair plants with pots is to have both with you at the time of your selection; the task is more difficult if you cannot see the two together. Like trying on clothing, you can place the plant (still in its nursery pot) into whatever container you are considering. A nursery's abundant inventory of both plants and pots makes it easy to experiment with contrast, repetition, texture, and more.

This yellow-green pot repeats the coloration of the lower part of the stems of *Euphorbia tirucalli* 'Sticks on Fire' (pencil plant). But might a different pot be a better choice?

A red pot emphasizes the red tips of 'Sticks on Fire' and also is a color complement to the plant's green stems.

An orange-glazed pot repeats, yet also contrasts with, a fancy ruffled echeveria that has teal blue leaves edged with orangey pink. Flora Grubb Gardens nursery, San Francisco, CA.

The overlapping leaves of graptopetalums look remarkably like the pot's pebbled surface. Seaside Gardens.

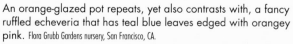

A pot with a metallic sheen emphasizes the metallic look of the aeonium's leaves. Art and Sandra Baldwin garden, San Diego, CA.

Sempervivums appear to grow in white baskets, but these are actually cast-concrete pots. Design by Molly Wood Garden Design, Costa Mesa, CA.

POT TYPES AND STYLES

The shapes and styles of pots that might hold succulents are limitless. The material need only be waterproof: terracotta, teak, china, glass, hypertufa, concrete, wrought iron, aluminum, fiberglass, resin, or plastic. It also is possible to use containers made of wire (heavy-gauge or filigree), lined with moss or coir to hold in the soil.

Since the choice of pot is primarily an aesthetic decision, a good place to begin is to define your home's style. If it is not obvious, pick one you like and use it consistently in accessories, indoors and out. Weathered wooden troughs suit a rustic timber house, for example, and metal cylinders a home with contemporary features.

Brightly glazed ceramic pots—which nurseries often group, rainbow-like, according to color, shape, and size—can make a patio, a sunroom, or

A palette of glazed pots.
Cambria Nursery and Florist, Cambria, CA.

any garden area cheerful and inviting. Succulents thrive in such containers, but keep in mind that dark colors absorb heat; in full sun, the soil in a thin-sided pot with a black or very dark glaze can be as much as 20 degrees warmer than the surrounding air.

Most succulents are shallow rooted, so unless you are planting a columnar cactus or a succulent tree, a pot of minimal depth should be fine. A container with a waist or that is a teardrop shape may not be a good choice; such pots may need to be broken at repotting time if roots have become a dense mass (commonly the case for sansevierias and agaves).

If a pot lacks drainage, the garden shop or nursery may be able to drill a hole for you. You can also make a drain hole yourself, using an electric drill with a masonry bit (be sure to wear eye protection). To protect flooring, a saucer may be necessary; set it atop pot feet so air can circulate beneath it. To keep soil from becoming soggy, elevate the pot by lining the saucer with pebbles.

Containers more than a few feet tall make a dynamic statement wherever you place them. Such pots tend to be expensive and difficult to move, so make sure that they can stay in the same location—and will look good there—for years. Because the addition of soil and plants makes a big container even heavier, position it where you want it prior to planting. If you need to relocate it as winter approaches, a dolly (handcart) is essential.

When choosing large pots, designers tend to prefer those with simple styles and silhouettes, and that are glazed or slightly textured but otherwise lack ornamentation. If temperatures in your area fall below 32 degrees F for extended periods, even large containers may crack when the soil they contain freezes and expands; better ones are reinforced with galvanized steel.

Pots made of clay, such as terracotta, vary from region to region because the material comes from the earth and no two sources are the same. Styles range from sleek and uncluttered to highly ornamented (such as a French jardinière with swags and cherubs) and everything in between. Clay pots have varying porosity, depending on the manufacturing method. Low-fired clay, though inexpensive, is not recommended, even if you apply a sealant. Though they provide good temporary homes for succulents, such pots slowly crumble, shedding dust that stains hardscape. And in a winter freeze, porous, moisture-laden clay pots may break—even if empty.

Succulents growing in natural stone and stone-look containers appear integral to their surroundings, as though emerging from a rocky outcropping. Such containers are traditionally used to house rock-garden succulents like stonecrop (sedums) and hen-and-chicks (sempervivums), but any small succulents look good in them.

You can make your own containers that resemble stone and that are lightweight, withstand freezing temperatures, retain moisture, and buffer roots from excess heat and cold. Hypertufa, long a tradition in Europe, is a mix of peat moss, perlite, and portland cement, plus reinforcing fibers. Similar to hypertufa is papercrete, which recycles paper waste. Papercrete consists of paper fiber, aggregate such as sand or perlite, and portland cement. Both hypertufa and papercrete, when wet, can be molded to a desired shape and size—generally a bowl or trough. How-to information for these can be found on the Web and in books and magazines, and classes in hypertufa or papercrete are occasionally offered by botanical gardens and horticultural organizations.

(top) Classic hypertufa troughs that are smooth and footed contain assorted sempervivums. Hampton Court Palace Flower Show, East Molesey, Surrey, England. Photo by Betty Mackey.

(bottom left) Italian terracotta containers alongside *Agave americana* 'Marginata'. Flora Grubb Gardens nursery.

(bottom right) Growing in what appears to be a rock from the garden are blue and green euphorbias and a small aloe. The pot is lightweight porous stone that has been cored. Solana Succulents nursery, Solana Beach, CA. Design by Jeff Moore.

Because of the popularity of homemade hypertufa and papercrete pots, fabricated pots with a similar look sometimes can be found in nurseries. This one contains *Echeveria subsessilis* and trailing *Senecio radicans* 'Fish Hooks'. Roger's Gardens nursery.

THE CLASSICAL LOOK

Containers with classical styling—which hearkens back to ancient Greece and Rome—include carved stone urns and troughs, and all manner of embellished clay and ceramic pots. Rounded and rosette succulents, such as aeoniums, echeverias, sempervivums, and graptopetalums, lend themselves to these romantic, ornamented containers. Pots with classical styling also effectively showcase plants with crisp, dynamic, upright lines, such as agaves and aloes.

Lithographs that date to the 1800s show agaves in classical urns—pots that sit atop a stem connected to a base. By raising the plants they contain, urns lend drama to upright succulents and provide vertical space for creeping plants to tumble. Graptopetalums and rat-tail cactus look good cascading from urns, and aeoniums or spherical succulents (such as barrel cacti) emphasize the containers' roundness.

A terracotta pot decorated with cherubs holds *Sedum morganianum* (donkey tail) and *Echeveria* 'Mexican Giant'. Duke Farms and Gardens, Hillsborough, NJ. Photo by Rob Cardillo.

A pedestal depicting the Greek god Atlas holds a pot that includes 'Afterglow' echeverias and dark green, slender-leaved *Agave stricta* (hedgehog agave). Living Green, San Francisco, CA. Design and photo by Davis Dalbok.

Green-and-red aeoniums appear to explode from a cast-iron urn. The backdrop is gray-green *Plectranthus argentatus*. Design by Sydney Baumgartner, Santa Barbara, CA.

The opulence of this urn is enhanced by tumbling grapetopetalums. R. C. and Beverly Cohen garden, Newport Beach, CA.

(right) Because of their weight, once in position and planted, carved stone urns become permanent fixtures. This one holds an aloe. Republic of San Marino, Europe. Photo by Frank Mitzel.

(left) What looks like a glazed ceramic pot is actually molded resin. Cathy Golden residence, San Diego, CA. Design by The Plant Man nursery.

(right) Slender *Euphorbia acrurensis* in a lightweight, faux-wood resin pot fills a vertical space. Suzy Schaefer residence, Rancho Santa Fe, CA.

Synthetic containers may so closely resemble those made of natural materials, it is impossible to tell the difference without tapping the pot or lifting it. Such pots tend to be lightweight—a definite advantage—but good ones may cost as much as their authentic counterparts, and inexpensive ones may fade or discolor over time.

If you live in a hot, arid region where the soil dries rapidly, you may want to grow succulents in nonporous containers that do not allow air exchange with the soil and therefore hold in precious moisture. But avoid white plastic. It is déclassé and allows light to penetrate the root zone, which can lead to algae growth. White plastic also tends to deteriorate rapidly—first noticeable when the rim of the pot cracks and breaks.

Concealing a nursery pot within an ornamental container can be both convenient and practical. By providing air space between the inner pot and the elements, a cachepot serves as a sweater in winter, and in summer, shades roots and keeps them cool. Use cachepots with drain holes so water does not puddle, or elevate inner pots atop stones.

STRAWBERRY JARS

Originally designed to hold strawberry plants, strawberry jars are vase-shaped vessels with cupped openings in their sides. For a billowy look, plant strawberry jars with sedums, graptopetalums, sempervivums, and other trailers. If you prefer a tighter composition that does not conceal the container, plant openings with rosette-shaped succulents such as echeverias.

Fill the jar with potting soil, then tuck cuttings into pockets and top. If transplanting potted succulents, start at the bottom and work your way up, adding plants and soil as you go. To fit plants into openings, trim root-balls. Gently pull them into the pot from the inside, then add more soil, tamping it around the roots. If the weight of the cutting or plant pulls it downward, wrap the stem with a collar of damp sphagnum moss to help anchor it.

In the top of the strawberry jar, you might add a plant that extends the lines of the composition upward and outward, such as an agave, aloe, or phormium. When you water the pot, make sure soil in the pockets is moistened.

As the hen-and-chicks rosettes of sempervivums multiply, they hug the outside of a strawberry jar. Pottmeyer garden, Wexford, PA. Photo by Rob Cardillo.

Cuttings in a white-glazed strawberry pot include a pink sedeveria, *Sedum furfuraceum*, and pale blue echeveria rosettes. Barbara Baker garden. Design by Chicweed.

A large strawberry pot planted solely with *Echeveria elegans* serves as a focal point for a garden of fine-textured foliage. Bob Clark garden, Oakland, CA. Photo by Charles Mann.

(left) A limited-edition pot by G. Wolff and Co. is stamped with the manufacturer's name and the year it was made. The succulent is *Echeveria secunda*. Barbara Baker garden.

(right) The blue pot was made by the Nelson McCoy Pottery Company in 1932; the orange pot, by the same company 30 years later. Collection of Karla Bonoff, Montecito, CA.

Purveyors of architectural antiques and garden art offer vintage containers of brightly glazed Fiestaware, and items made by Bauer Pottery and McCoy Pottery. Crisp-lined agaves and aloes are particularly suited to streamlined, midcentury-modern pots with geometric shapes and nicknames based on what they resemble, such as avocado and wok; one manufacturer is Architectural Pottery. Rosette succulents show to advantage in retro-looking containers that are simple to the point of austerity, such as those from G. Wolff and Co. of Connecticut.

For one-of-a-kinds, go with artist-designed pots; wonderful ones can be found at succulent shows and specialty nurseries. Once you find an artist whose style pleases you, his or her work will lend unity and personality to your home and garden. Or why not take a pottery class and create your own?

(top left) A windowsill pot's ridged rim echoes the texture of *Mammillaria polythele*. Sculpture and design by Erik Gronborg, Solana Beach, CA.

(top right) *Sansevieria cylindrica* appears to plunge into this handcrafted pot. Enhancing the composition is a top-dressing of crushed yellow glass. California Cactus Center nursery. Design by Arree Thongthiraj. Pot by Mike Cone.

Haworthia attenuata 'Variegata' and *Crassula perforata* grow in an artist-designed pot with a crackle glaze. Design by Diane Dunhill, Santa Barbara, CA. Pot by Charles Varni of Plantera Primal, Oceano, CA.

Collecting miniature containers gives me an excuse to explore antique stores, garden boutiques, and secondhand shops. Such objects are seldom expensive, make good souvenirs, and fit easily into a suitcase. Diminutive pots can also be found at craft and floral supply stores, sold in multiples—which is helpful if you want to repeat them along a windowsill or use them for party favors.

Keep in mind that miniature arrangements need to be watered more often than typical container gardens. The smaller the pot, the less soil and moisture it can hold, and the more quickly it will dry out.

Flowers of *Sedum dasyphyllum* 'Lilac Mound' are delicate pink and about ⅛ inch in diameter. The metal container is about the size of a butter dish. Flora Grubb Gardens nursery.

(top left) Juvenile *Haworthia pumila* fits a Lilliputian pot. The topdressing of coarse sand is in scale with the composition. California Cactus Center nursery.

(top right) Tiny pots on a 3-inch-square mat hold cuttings that resemble the parent plants. Terra Sol Garden Center, Santa Barbara, CA. Design by Margarita Huerta.

A red plastic doll's shoe makes a whimsical container for tiny rosette succulents. The cuttings were inserted into holes poked into tightly packed moss. EuroAmerican Propagators, Bonsall, CA. Design by Margee Rader.

The shell's fluted edge repeats the shape of crested *Euphorbia lactea* 'Variegata'. Inter-City Cactus and Succulent Show, Los Angeles County Arboretum. Design by Larry Grammer.

A handful of glass florist's marbles sets off a simple composition of a clam shell and two *Echeveria* 'Perle von Nurnberg' rosettes. California Cactus Center nursery.

Shells make intriguing containers for succulents, and stores that specialize in pots sell large cast-concrete or plaster ones. Choose succulents that complement the shape of the container and suggest undersea flora, such as sedums, euphorbias, and echeverias.

(top left) A cast-stone sconce planted with *Sempervivum arachnoideum* gives this romantic figure tight curls that will become more abundant over time. Plantplay Nursery, Carlsbad, CA.

(top right) Lady-head ceramic containers from the 1930s to the 1950s are highly collectible. *Aeonium* 'Kiwi' rosettes suggest a floral headdress. Collection of R. C. and Beverly Cohen.

Growing out of the top of this fish flowerpot, resembling curly hair, is *Sedum rubrotinctum*. Sculpture and design by Jolee Pink, Encinitas, CA.

A pot shaped like a head or an animal, or a sconce with a face, may look odd empty but when filled with rosette-forming or trailing succulents— or perhaps a bristly cactus—makes a delightful presentation. Rather than positioning face pots prominently, I like to put them where guests will happen upon them; the discovery invariably elicits a laugh or comment. But do resist the temptation to go overboard—a little whimsy goes a long way.

FLEA-MARKET FINDS

Succulents will grow in antique china, wooden boxes, and even baking dishes, given adequate room for a little soil and/or tightly packed sphagnum moss. Sources include antique stores, garage and yard sales, secondhand and thrift shops, import stores, and flea markets. (Containers exposed to rain or frequent irrigation must have drainage.)

(top) An old flour sifter holds aeoniums and jade. EuroAmerican Propagators. Design by Margee Rader.

A teacup planted with echeverias and secured atop a painted post adds whimsy to a flower bed. Kathy LaFleur garden, Rancho Santa Fe, CA.

(bottom) Feathers of a china hen include crassula and aeonium cuttings. Mon Petit Chou, Encinitas, CA. Design by Bonnie Manion.

A china bowl holds cuttings that grow in tightly packed sphagnum moss. Variegated *Sedum lineare* sparkles in the foreground. EuroAmerican Propagators. Design by Margee Rader.

A child's fire engine is planted with sedum cuttings. Flower Girls, Encinitas, CA. Design by Bette Childs.

Echeveria rosettes populate a muffin tin. Chicweed.

A rusty toy wagon makes a shabby-chic container for an eclectic assortment of succulents. Out of the Blue, Solana Beach, CA. Design by Debi Beard.

EMBELLISHMENTS

It may not be the pot or the succulents it contains that lend magic to a composition, but rather the addition of a decorative element to the pot itself, or alongside it—perhaps a figurine, seashell, glazed tile, or intriguing rusty object.

In selecting embellishments, aim to complete a vignette, so that the pot, its contents, and the setting look right together. If you aspire to whimsy—to make people exclaim with delight—keep the finished composition uncluttered and avoid anything trite. If you are uncertain whether the addition works, leave it for a day or so, then come back and evaluate it afresh.

(left) A blue glass ball repeats the blue of the tile behind it, tying in the potted euphorbia with its backdrop. Design by Jim Bishop, Bishop Garden Design, San Diego, CA.

(right) A pair of brass turtles adds interest to aeoniums in terracotta pots on stair risers. Suzy Schaefer garden.

(top left) Chunks of blue glass lend bling to *Aeonium arboreum* 'Zwartkop' rosettes. Photo and design by Davis Dalbok.

(top right) In a composition enhanced by slag glass, the container's shape echoes that of *Crassula perfoliata* var. *falcata* (propeller plant). The Plant Man nursery. Design by Michael Buckner.

A figurine with a blue ruffled dress echoes the shape and colors of echeverias nearby; appropriately, on the left is *Echeveria* 'Party Dress'. Peggy Petitmermet garden.

TOPDRESSING

An important but often overlooked design element—one that offers contrast, repetition, color, and texture—is a pot's topdressing, or mulch. This finishing touch is generally a nonporous material that allows air exchange with roots through the soil's top layer and keeps perlite in the soil from floating away.

The selection of a topdressing might be inspired by the plants, their container, or the setting. When used consistently, the same or similar topdressing will unify disparate containers. To create a palette of topdressings, nursery owners and designers buy coarse sand, pea gravels, pebbles, and crushed rock in bulk from suppliers of landscape materials.

For a simple, sophisticated look—and one preferred by judges at cactus and succulent shows—go with a natural crushed rock that is tan, brown, black, gray, rust-red, or a barley-like blend. Southern California collectors who participate in shows hike the Mojave and Borrego deserts in search of

A natural topdressing and rocks do not call attention to themselves yet enhance a design that showcases variegated haworthias. *California Cactus Center nursery. Design by Larry Grammer.*

(left) Peach-colored crushed glass repeats a color found in the variegation of the phormium, the leaf edges of *Sedum nussbaumerianum*, and the pale terracotta of the pot—unifying all three. Lunenfeld garden. Design by Laura Morton.

(right) Cat's-eye marbles repeat the shapes of spiky cacti and contrast with their texture. Evelyn Jacob and Mindy Rosenblatt garden, Santa Barbara, CA.

coarse sand and decomposed granite with good texture and color. They sift what they find—using screens of different sizes—to glean uniform pebbles and grains, and gather "already sifted" material from the tops of anthills. Collectors also bring back rocks that match the color of the topdressing, or with pleasing shapes, textures, or striations.

Colorful topdressings make otherwise bland containers stand out and, when used skillfully, can introduce an element of whimsy. Tumbled glass and marbles (flattened as well as spherical) come in a variety of hues and are sold by the scoop, ounce, or bagful at design-oriented garden stores and floral supply shops. Fine, glossy gravels from pet shops that sell aquarium supplies are yet another option.

When in doubt, err on the side of subtlety. Unless there is a compositional reason (for example, you want the soil to appear snow-covered), a stark white topdressing—or one that similarly shouts—will detract from plants you had hoped to show to advantage. And as you experiment with topdressings, keep in mind that the finer the gravel, the more difficult it will be to remove.

To keep potting soil from coming up through the topdressing when the pot is watered, add a layer of sand between the two.

TEN QUICK AND EASY PLANT-POT COMBOS

1. For color repetition and texture contrast, plant a coppery-spined cactus in a terracotta pot. Top dress with bits of broken terracotta or a similarly orange-toned crushed rock. Here, spines of a small parodia repeat the color of its pot as well as the gravel topdressing. Three textures—bristly, smooth, and chunky—contrast with one another. Cactus Jungle nursery, Berkeley, CA. Design by Hap Hollibaugh.

2. In a multiplant combo in a pink pot, include an echeveria that has a pink blush. The pink container will make the pink in the echeveria rosette pop, and it will tie the composition together. Vivai Piante Schiavo nursery, Abano Terme, Italy. Photo by Frank Mitzel.

3. Plant a medusa-form euphorbia in a spherical pot. The euphorbia's octopus-like leaves will echo the roundness of the pot, and the plant's bumpy texture will contrast with the pot's smooth surface. This round pot emphasizes the cylindrical shape of *Euphorbia flanaganii*. Yellow flowers contrast with the pot's bright blue glaze. Design by Jim Bishop.

4. Pair green sempervivums that have red-tipped leaves with a red-glazed pot. The composition here is enhanced by the juxtaposition of complementary colors. Barrels & Branches nursery.

5. Place a succulent with beadlike leaves in or near an object embellished with beads. Beads and shells on this pot repeat the shape and color of *Sedum burrito* leaves, as does a mat of green glass beads. Whitney Green garden, Santa Monica, CA.

6. Combine magenta-black *Aeonium arboreum* 'Zwartkop' with a yellow-glazed pot. The dark aeonium, which suggests a glossy flower, echoes the shiny surface of its container and contrasts with its color. Art and Sandra Baldwin garden.

7. Allow a fine-textured sedum to cascade naturally from a small bonsai pot atop a pedestal; the simple composition, reminiscent of Japanese paintings of pendant pines or wisteria, will present a similarly elegant, flowing structure. Here a palm-sized clay pot of *Sedum spathulifolium* sits on a tiny pedestal. Bonsai Society of San Francisco. Design by Eric Schrader.

8. Plant an echeveria in a bowl-shaped container. The pot is the succulent's shape in reverse, so plant and pot combine to form a sphere. In this composition, the teal of the leaves of *Echeveria* 'Morning Light' repeats the verdigris glaze of its pot, and the pot's shape mirrors that of the plant. Pot and design by John Bleck, Santa Barbara, CA.

9. Place your collection in matching pots that repeat or contrast with the color and texture of a nearby wall. This weathered brick wall is the color complement of cobalt blue containers that each hold an assortment of echeverias and sempervivums. West Green House Gardens, Hampshire, England. Photo by Andrea Jones.

10. Repeat a pot's cross-hatch pattern with succulents that have pointed leaves. For example, the leaves and orange flowers of *Echeveria* 'Doris Taylor' echo elements found in the pattern of a talavera pot. Seaside Gardens. Design by Sam Maybery.

Sedum sieboldii is a graceful cascader. Flora Grubb Gardens nursery, San Francisco, CA.

Part Two

PLANT PALETTE

This sunset jade (*Crassula ovata* 'Hummel's Sunset') has been in the same pot for 20 years and has naturally bonsai'd. If grown in the ground for the same period, in optimal conditions, it might be a sofa-sized shrub. San Marcos Growers, Santa Barbara, CA. Design by Randy Baldwin.

What follows is a fashion show: a selection of cacti and succulents supremely suited to container culture—and to container *couture*. Strutting down the runway are plants that are lovely in their own right and that are ideal for enhancing pot groupings and multiplant arrangements. The majority are available from specialty nurseries, garden centers, and online vendors. (If you cannot find the plant locally, enter its botanical name into an Internet search engine.) Included are a few that are uncommon yet deserve wider recognition; where this is the case, I have noted it.

Unless otherwise specified, succulents described here require well-drained soil that goes nearly dry between waterings, along with protection from excessive rain, humidity, damp cold, and scorching sun (especially if the leaves are variegated). These plants are frost tender and winter dormant, and their primary growth period is spring; they may slow down in the heat of summer and then spurt again as temperatures cool in the fall. They prefer to be outdoors, weather permitting, but can be cultivated indoors if they receive adequate light and air circulation.

Shrub and tree succulents (and many that form rosettes) grow more slowly in pots than comparable plants in the garden or in habitat. Like goldfish, many cacti and succulents cease growing when they reach the size that their containers will comfortably accommodate. As the plant naturally bonsais, its leaves may become proportionately smaller. This is not extraordinary; in nature, two seedlings the same age may develop quite differently. One with roots confined in a crevice will be more diminutive than—though as healthy as—a sibling nearby in ample soil.

Additional factors that influence a succulent's growth rate and eventual size include light conditions, quantity and frequency of water, fertilizer (or lack of it), and amount and duration of heat or cold.

SUCCULENTS FOR CONTAINERS

Aeoniums

Pinwheel leaves of aeoniums form a daisylike silhouette. The center leaves are the new growth, and as the rosette ages, the oldest (outer) leaves wither and fall off. Consequently, the stem supporting the rosette becomes exposed and elongates over time. Aeonium rosettes work well in floral-style compositions and are effective arranged in rows to create geometric designs. Use tall aeoniums to provide height at the center or back of an arrangement, and short-stemmed rosettes for foreground interest. As aeonium stems lengthen, they will deconstruct a tight arrangement and make a loosely structured one even airier. To refresh a composition, snap off the rosettes along with an inch or two of stem, then reinsert in the pot so stems anchor the cuttings. Leaves may droop a bit at first but will regain their vigor once roots take hold. The old trunk may sprout new rosettes from leaf axils, but this does not always happen; if the denuded stem is unsightly, remove it.

Most aeoniums are green, but colorful ones are available and well worth seeking. *Aeonium* 'Sunburst', which is striped with yellow and may be edged in pink, is among the loveliest of succulents. It resembles a large flower and because of its light color stands out against darker foliage. *Aeonium* 'Garnet' is one of several cultivars that are green in the center and red on the leaf tips; the most striking are cherry red. *Aeonium arboreum* 'Zwartkop' appears

(left) A red pot makes red on the leaf tips of *Aeonium* 'Sunburst' pop. Tropic World nursery, Escondido, CA.

(right) Over the past decade, my pot of *Aeonium arboreum* 'Zwartkop' has become an odd display of curved and pendant stems. The name comes from *schwarz*, the German word for black.

black at first glance but is actually deep magenta, which becomes evident when the plant is backlit. 'Zwartkop' is indeed captivating, but keep in mind it tends to disappear, visually, in bouquetlike arrangements because it reads as a dark spot or hole. Give 'Zwartkop' a solid backdrop or juxtapose it with plants with bright yellow or silvery foliage, such as *Crassula ovata* 'Hummel's Sunset' or *Helichrysum petiolare*. For a pleasing repetition of color, grow purple-tipped *Aeonium arboreum* var. *atropurpureum* and hybrids of 'Zwartkop' with green centers, in lime green or chartreuse pots.

Aeonium tabuliforme (lily pad aeonium) has nearly flat green rosettes, with each leaf delicately fringed with short white hairs. This aeonium can be tricky to grow; give it exceptionally well-drained soil, good air circulation, filtered light, and virtually no summer water. The head can get about 15 inches in diameter yet stays low to the ground, making it vulnerable to rot.

Aeonium haworthii, which has gray-green rosettes consisting of short, pointed, wedge-shaped leaves, forms a multibranched, mounded shrublet. If you live where frost or extreme heat are not concerns, grow *Aeonium haworthii* in your garden to provide an abundant source of 3-inch-diameter (and smaller) rosettes for use in wreaths and topiaries. Similar in size and shape is *Aeonium* 'Kiwi', a smaller shrub with yellow-and-green leaves edged with red.

When an aeonium blooms, the center of the rosette elongates into a conical or dome-shaped multiblossomed flower that is yellow, cream, or red-

New leaves at the center of *Aeonium canariense* rosettes are framed by progressively larger, older leaves. Art and Sandra Baldwin garden, San Diego, CA.

Flat rosettes of *Aeonium tabuliforme* (lily pad aeonium) in nursery pots appear to float. Succulent Gardens nursery, Castroville, CA.

dish. The rosette dies after flowering, but aeoniums will go for years without blooming, and not all in a clump or on a shrub do so at once, so the loss is not significant. These are wonderful cut flowers. Every spring, I place 2-foot-long flower spikes of aeoniums from my garden in a tall, vase-shaped pot. Even without water, they look good for weeks.

From the Canary Islands off the west coast of North Africa, aeoniums like slightly more moisture than other succulents. They are understory plants; if possible, grow them in bright shade. The darker the leaves, the greater the sun tolerance. Aeoniums are summer-dormant winter growers.

Agaves

Agaves are easy-care, New World succulents that tolerate less-than-ideal conditions. With the notable exception of *Agave attenuata*, which forms a trunk over time, most are stemless rosettes. All have tapered leaves that spiral outward and upward. Some agaves resemble artichokes, others a bouquet of bayonets. Leaves, which generally are concave, vary in shape from wedges to whips.

Spikes at leaf tips and along margins, as well as possibly toxic sap, make these keep-away plants, unfriendly to children, pets, and careless gardeners. Even so, my appreciation for agaves continues to grow. I like those with sharklike teeth and enjoy looking for the shadowy imprints these have made on inner leaves.

Agaves may not be for everyone, but from a design standpoint, their crisp forms are unmatched. They have long been thought of as enormous plants, and certainly that is true of *Agave americana* (century plant), which grows effortlessly throughout the Southwest and is found in gardens worldwide. Better for pot culture is cream-and-gray-striped tuxedo agave (*Agave americana* 'Mediopicta Alba'), which seldom gets taller than 4 feet. Many more species of *Agave* exist, and in response to increased demand, small agaves ideal for containers are becoming widely available.

Agaves reproduce from seeds, and some also produce bulbils (plantlets that form along the bloom stalk) or pups (new plants from lateral roots) that can be pulled loose and potted. Almost all agaves are monocarpic (they flower once and then die), but it takes years for agaves to bloom, and when they do, it is an event, because the bloom spikes are magnificent, and large in proportion to the plant. Container-grown agaves generally take much longer to flower than those in the ground.

A 3-foot-diameter terracotta pot holds *Agave* 'Joe Hoak' surrounded by 'Afterglow' echeverias coming into bloom. Cascading over the side is *Senecio radicans* 'Fish Hooks'. Sherman Gardens, Corona del Mar, CA. Design by Matthew Maggio.

The beast has beauty: *Agave bovicornuta* (cow's horn agave) glows when backlit. Phil Favell garden, Elfin Forest CA.

Even though pot culture naturally stunts agaves, their roots can be remarkably strong and vigorous. A concern with confining immature versions of large agaves (such as *Agave americana*, *Agave franzosinii*, and *Agave vilmoriniana*) in pots is that their roots swell quickly and put pressure on the container, which subsequently cracks.

If you want to keep a potentially large agave potted, you will need to do some root pruning. Once a year or so (ideally as the plant emerges from winter dormancy), slide the agave out of its container, wash the roots, and cut them in half straight across. Then repot—no need to let them heal.

When grooming agaves, snip sharp leaf tips to protect yourself and others from impalement. Remove any dirt or debris that falls into an agave's crown, lest these harbor moisture and pests. If you must trim an overlarge agave, preserve its symmetry by cutting the leaves flush with the stem rather

Agave victoriae-reginae. Ruth Bancroft Garden, Walnut Creek, CA.

Mangave 'Macho Mocha'. The Plant Man nursery, San Diego, CA.

than truncating them part way. To remove a marred or withered leaf, cut off the tip, split the leaf lengthwise, then separate the two halves; they should pull out easily. Most agaves do best in full sun; they will adapt to part shade but will lean toward light. Soft-leaved *Agave attenuata* needs protection from frost and harsh sun.

Most agaves are hardy to the mid-to-high 20s, and some go much lower. The genus is remarkably diverse, with species found in habitat from sea level to 9000 feet. One January in the Denver Botanic Gardens, I observed a 2-foot-diameter *Agave parryi* blanketed with snow, with only its tips showing. This fairly common agave tolerates temperatures to −20 degrees F; it is a large gray artichoke with minimally toothed leaves tipped in black. Subspecies 'Truncata' (to 15 degrees F) has wider leaves and a more spherical form; it shows to advantage in a round container that echoes its shape.

SMALL AGAVES

Small agaves once considered rare are becoming readily available. Those included here are showy and make excellent container plants.

Agave 'Blue Glow'. Blue-green leaves have subtle, watercolor-like color striations and red-orange margins.

Agave chiapensis. Broad green leaves that taper like minarets are lined with small black prickles.

Agave colorata. Leaves are light gray, patterned with white; margins are strongly toothed.

Agave filifera. White filaments curl away from the edges of dark green leaves.

Agave geminiflora. Thin, narrow, flexible leaves that may have fibrous, silvery hairs along leaf margins form a pincushion.

Agave ghiesbreghtii. Dark green leaves have a brushed-looking, lighter green variegation down the middle.

Agave gypsophila. Wavy and curled gray leaves appear trimmed with pinking shears.

Agave horrida. A compact rosette has toothed leaves reminiscent of those of Venus flytrap.

Agave marmorata. Pale blue-gray leaves are wide and lobed, with orange tips.

Agave montana. Toothed leaves end in long terminal spines that make the plant, at first glance, appear to sparkle. Cultivar 'Baccarat', which has short and broad gray-green leaves, is so named because the impressions made on the leaves suggest the facets of Baccarat crystal.

Agave parryi 'Cream Spike'. With cream-striped leaves margined in dark brown, this agave grows to a mere 4 inches tall by about 6 inches wide. Hardy to the midteens.

Agave potatorum. Blue-gray leaves are lined with orange teeth; terminal spines are long and wavy.

Agave 'Blue Glow'. Sunshine Gardens nursery, Encinitas, CA.

Agave potatorum.

Agave pumila. Short, fat leaves with dark striations have sharp terminal spines.

Agave stricta (hedgehog agave). Whiplike, toothless (but sharply pointed) leaves grow into dense clumps that resemble cowlicks.

Other hardy agaves include toothy green *Agave gentryi* 'Jaws' (to 5 degrees F), silvery gray *Agave montana* (to −10 degrees F), pale gray *Agave neomexicana* (to −20 degrees F), and *Agave utahensis* (to −10 degrees F), which has narrow, serrated leaves. An excellent cabbage-sized agave that tolerates temperatures into the teens is *Agave victoriae-reginae*, which has dark green leaves outlined in white, with black tips. Similar to this small agave is its slightly larger consort, *Agave victoriae-reginae* var. *ferdinandi-regis*, which is dark gray-green with V-shaped white markings that appear drawn with chalk.

Surging in popularity with collectors and garden designers are mangaves, hybrids between agaves and manfredas. Plants look like delicate agaves with speckled leaves. *Mangave* 'Macho Mocha' (introduced by Yucca Do Nursery in Texas) has gray-green leaves covered with brown-purple spots. Mangaves' soft leaves are easily damaged, which can spoil the look of the plants, so grow them in a protected location and check often for snails and other pests.

Closely related to agaves are furcraeas, which have a similar upright habit and silhouette. The showiest is yellow-variegated *Furcraea foetida* var. *medio-picta*; give it full sun only in mild maritime locations, and dappled shade elsewhere lest its leaves burn.

Aloes

Aloes are native to South Africa, the Arabian peninsula, and Madagascar. They range from a few inches in diameter to large trees, and their thick, lancelike leaves are smooth, bumpy, or prickled, usually with toothed margins. In general, aloes like slightly wetter conditions than agaves. The majority of aloes commonly in cultivation need summer water, but a few cannot tolerate it; if this is the case, I have noted it.

Frost may burn the tips of aloe leaves, causing them to shrivel, and most aloes cannot handle a hard freeze. One exception is *Aloe striatula*, which is hardy to 15 degrees F; it has slender leaves and bright yellow flowers late fall through winter. Clumps grow to 3 or 4 feet tall and spread (in the garden) to about 6 feet wide.

At first glance, aloes and agaves look alike, but the differences are significant: aloes have gel-filled leaves, while those of agaves are fibrous. Agaves are New World succulents; aloes are from the Old World. The terminal spines and teeth of agaves are a different and denser tissue than the rest of the leaf, whereas the prickles of aloes are extensions of leaf tissue—and may

Aloe nobilis rosettes baked by sun are redder than those beneath them in semishade. University of California Botanical Garden, Berkeley, CA.

At upwards of 6 feet tall when in bloom, *Aloe marlothii* is a dramatic choice for large containers. Desert Theater nursery.

be all over the leaf (agaves have them only at tips and edges). And unlike agaves, which die after blooming, aloes flower annually. Many do so in mid-winter, their torchlike flowers lending hot hues to nurseries, greenhouses, and gardens. Tubular blooms are arrayed on leafless, sometimes branching stems.

About a third of aloe species form trunks over time; the rest are acaules-cent (stemless). These may be solitary, or they may form offsets that crowd each other as they clump or creep. Leaf colors range from shades of blue to yellow-green. Many redden when sun baked or stressed. (A succulent that is stressed has received more cold or sun than it needs, and/or less water. Such less-than-ideal growing conditions, though not harmful, may cause green leaves to turn shades of orange, red, or brown.) Add to this variegates that are striped or mottled, and aloes are arguably the most colorful succulents.

Aloe polyphylla. Carolyn Schaer garden. Design by Michael Buckner.

Rocks enhance a composition that features diminutive aloes with a bumpy texture. Sunshine Gardens nursery, Encinitas, CA. Design by Howard Vieweg.

Aloes that turn color when given full sun include *Aloe cameronii* (crimson), *Aloe buhrii* (orange), and *Aloe taurii* and *Aloe dorotheae* (bright red). Softball-sized *Aloe nobilis*, which forms dark green rosettes with wedge-shaped leaves toothed with white or yellow prickles, turns shades of red-orange.

Worth looking for are lovely variegates of *Aloe nobilis* and *Aloe arborescens*, which have yellow-striped leaves. Blue-green *Aloe brevifolia* resembles *Aloe nobilis* but has shorter leaves that do not redden. *Aloe microstigma* has teal-and-rose leaves dotted with white; *Aloe elgonica*, green rosettes that blush rose-purple at their centers; and *Aloe variegata* (partridge breast aloe), bold zigzag-striped leaves that form V-shaped stacks.

Creeping aloes suitable for hanging baskets include fast-growing *Aloe ciliaris*, with slender, widely spaced, lancelike leaves fringed with white; *Aloe juvenna*, with small, white-prickled, triangular, tightly-stacked green leaves that turn orange when stressed; *Aloe perfoliata* (syn. *Aloe mitriformis*), with smooth blue-green leaves that blush rosy purple; and *Aloe distans* (jeweled aloe), with wedge-shaped leaves and distinctive yellow prickles.

Aloe vera (syn. *Aloe barbadensis*) is among the best-known aloes and one of the most widely cultivated; it is a windowsill plant in many homes because the gel within its leaves soothes burns and other skin irritations. *Aloe vera*, though one of the juiciest, is not the only medicinal aloe. To access an aloe's translucent, glutinous gel, snap off a leaf and peel away the skin. The gel has cosmetic uses as well; Cleopatra reputedly used it as a skin-refreshing facial mask.

Large aloes, such as *Aloe marlothii* and *Aloe ferox*, are dramatic in large outdoor pots. *Aloe arborescens*, the most common garden aloe in the Southwest, makes a good filler plant but is clump forming and may not bloom until too ungainly for its container. Tree *Aloe bainesii* can stay in a pot for a year or two but prefers to be in the ground. Slow-growing *Aloe plicatilis* has flat leaves that look like fans of popsicle sticks. It has a treelike branching structure and serves well as a tall succulent for arrangements—provided the potting medium is kept dry (or nearly so) in summer.

Aloes look good grown solo, especially when the container plays off of hues in the plant's leaves. *Aloe striata* (coral aloe) is among the most popular for pot culture; it stays a manageable size (to 18 inches high and as wide) and has smooth, orange-margined teal leaves.

More diminutive (6 inches high) are new hybrids with exceptional color and texture; some have leaves encrusted with what look like splinters and come in shades of red, brown, orange, or cream (*Aloe* 'Lizard Lips' is one example). Hybridizers include John Bleck of Santa Barbara; Dick Wright of Fallbrook, CA; and Kelly Griffin of Rancho Soledad Nurseries in Rancho Santa Fe, CA. Many of the new small aloes are tissue cultured and sold under the Proven Winners label.

An intriguing bigeneric (derived from two different genera) cross between an aloe and a gasteria, created by Griffin, is ×*Gasteraloe* 'Midnight'. The plant has stiff leaves so uniformly covered with whitish bumps that it appears salted. When grown in bright shade, it is green; in full sun, brownish red.

Another aloe gaining popularity is *Aloe* 'Rooikappie' (an Afrikaans word pronounced "roy-copy"). From the nursery of South African horticulturist Cynthia Giddy (now deceased), it is bright green, stays small (to 12 inches in diameter), and—unlike most aloes—blooms repeatedly. The Huntington Botanical Gardens reports, "There seems to be no month of the year when some flowers are not present on *Aloe* 'Rooikappie' in our nursery or garden." The salmon-colored blooms are yellow tipped.

Aloe polyphylla (spiral aloe) has wedge-shaped leaves that form a distinctive clockwise or counterclockwise whorl (collectors covet one of each). In its native habitat—the high mountains of Lesotho, South Africa—*Aloe polyphylla* grows in crevices on steep basalt slopes, anchored by an aggressive root system that is continually bathed by rainfall or runoff. Atypical of the genus, this aloe tolerates snow and below-freezing temperatures (to 10 degrees F) and is difficult to cultivate in dry, hot climates. Plants will suffer when summer heat exceeds 90 degrees F (temperatures much cooler than that are best). Soil should stay moist yet drain rapidly; grow *Aloe polyphylla* in a coarse mix of two-thirds potting soil and one-third lava rock, pumice, or perlite. Set the plant high in its container so the lowest leaves are above the rim. For best form, provide six to eight hours of bright light daily, ideally morning sun. Do not remove older leaves on the underside unless they are paper thin; their deterioration is essential to the health of the plant.

Bulbines

An easy-care succulent excellent for containers (though not often seen in them) is *Bulbine frutescens*, which forms clumps of upright, apple-green leaves 12 to 18 inches tall. These send up spaghetti-thin flower spikes tipped with cones of delicate yellow flowers. Cultivar 'Hallmark' has orange and yellow blooms and is smaller overall than the species.

Bulbine frutescens 'Hallmark' shares a pot with trailing *Lotus berthelotii* (parrot's beak). Seaside Gardens, Carpinteria, CA.

Cacti

Numerous cacti do well in containers, both solo and in combinations, provided that their requirements for minimal water, exceptionally fast-draining soil, warmth, and excellent air circulation are met. Most prefer hot, dry conditions, but some tolerate temperatures well below zero. Although their native habitat may be desert, the majority of cacti (at least when small) grow in the shelter and shade of larger plants.

Spines on cacti are modified leaves designed to protect the plants from foraging animals and extremes of sun, heat, and cold. In form, cacti are spherical or columnar, or have jointed pads. Cacti ribbed like accordions inhabit regions where rain falls intensely and then not at all for months; when drenched, the plants plump, then they slowly contract as drought requires them to drain their reserves. Contraction also enables the plants to shade themselves, thereby inhibiting desiccation; the deeper the grooves, the less sun reaches the skin.

Allow cacti to crowd their pots. Roots that fill a container will keep soil drier, and unused potting medium may hold too much moisture for these desert dwellers. Broken or damaged roots are particularly susceptible to rot, so wait a week before watering newly transplanted cacti.

Mammillaria is the largest and most widely collected genus of spherical cacti. These eventually form colonies and wear crowns of dainty flowers in spring. *Mammillaria plumosa*, one of the few pettable cacti, grows into a loose mound of balls coated with soft, asterisk-like white spines. Plants in another popular genus of globular cacti, *Rebutia*, produce neon-bright flowers in shades of magenta, orange, or crimson. *Echinocactus grusonii* (golden barrel cactus) forms highly textural spheres covered with overlapping yellow spines. Many species of *Ferocactus*, another genus of barrels, have red spines that when backlit, appear ablaze.

Astrophytums, which have ribs outlined with dots of flocking, suggest plump stars, especially when viewed from above. Parodias (also known as notocactus) grow contentedly in windowsill pots for years; *Parodia magnifica* has deep furrows and golden spines. Gymnocalyciums also are globular; depending on the species, their exteriors may form pillowy bumps each centered with a starburst of spines. Echinopsis (or trichocereus) are spherical when young, columnar as they age; they produce large, showy, satiny flowers.

My earliest memory of cactus—and doubtless I am not alone in this—is of a painful encounter with *Opuntia ficus-indica* (prickly pear), which has pads as thick as potholders and needlelike spines. Though treacherous, the

Mammillaria elongata.  Mary Rodriguez garden, Rancho Santa Fe, CA.

Rebutia heliosa in bloom. San Diego Cactus and Succulent Society.

(top) Assorted cacti include mammillarias, parodias, cereus, and in the foreground, ferocactus and golden barrels (*Echinocactus grusonii*). Succulent Gardens nursery.

Opuntia ficus-indica forms a backdrop for a grouping that includes barrel cacti and *Agave victoriae-reginae.* The Living Desert, Palm Desert, CA.

plants are not unlovely, and nothing connotes a desert garden like their ping-pong paddles. Smooth (or nearly so) kinds do exist; one introduced by noted botanist Luther Burbank in the early part of the 20th century is *Opuntia ficus-indica* 'Burbank Spineless'. Also appealing, and much smaller, is *Opuntia microdasys* (bunny ears); plants are polka-dotted with gold, brown, or white tufts. Unfortunately, these consist of glochids (small, irritating spines) that detach at the slightest touch.

Ceroids (*Cereus* and similar genera) are columnar; the name means "torch." Flowers in shades of pink, cream, or white are showy but short lived; egg-shaped or oblong fruit follow. Grow ceroids in deep pots with rocks in the bottom for stability. Depending on the species, a 6-inch plant may grow an additional 18 inches in a year. A ceroid often sold in nurseries is *Pachycereus marginatus* (Mexican fence post). *Cereus peruvianus* monstrose form, with its flowing, bumpy texture, resembles a melting candle. *Myrtillocactus geometrizans* branches repeatedly to form a shrub as wide as it is tall. Blue ceroids such as *Pilosocereus pachycladus* have golden or coppery spines that contrast beautifully with their azure skin. Most are highly sensitive to cold.

Woolly cacti, on the other hand, wear natural sweaters that protect them when temperatures drop (many are from mountainous habitats). *Cephalocereus senilis*, commonly called old man cactus, is shrouded with what looks like white beard; *Oreocereus* has toothpick-like spines that protrude through white filaments; and *Cleistocactus strausii* bristles with short white hairs. All are gorgeous backlit.

Rat-tail cactus (*Disocactus flagelliformis*, syn. *Aporocactus flagelliformis*) resembles long, fuzzy ropes. The plants are weirdly beautiful in hanging baskets and pedestal pots. Provide a minimum temperature of 43 degrees F; bright, indirect light; and a fairly rich potting mix. Repot every other year in fresh soil, even though the plants may not have outgrown their pots. In winter, trim old, discolored stems (cut at the base) to make way for spring growth.

(left) A green ceramic pot with a basketweave pattern emphasizes the textured surface of a gymnocalycium and also repeats its color.

(right) One of the blue ceroids: *Micranthocereus dolichospermaticus*. Buck Hemenway garden, Riverside, CA.

Hardy cacti

Cold-hardy cacti that can spend the winter outdoors (if kept dry or nearly so) include these:

Coryphantha and *Escobaria*. These small, globular cacti have dark green skin beneath an overlapping tracery of spiderlike spines. Satiny flowers in warm colors emerge from the top of the plant. *Escobaria vivipara* (to −20 degrees F) has large blooms ranging from shades of purple to light pink.

Echinocereus. Numerous species of this genus of hedgehog cacti are hardy to well below 0 degrees F. *Echinocereus reichenbachii* (to −25 degrees F) tolerates more moisture than most; its common name, lace cactus, is derived from the plant's delicate-looking, overlapping rows of spines. The species offers a wide range of forms and flower colors, including bright rose-pink. *Echinocereus fendleri* (Fendler's hedgehog cactus, to −20 degrees F) is also worth seeking, as are claret cup cacti *Echinocereus coccineus* and *Echinocereus polyacanthus* (both to −20 degrees F).

Opuntia. Widely cultivated *Opuntia humifusa* (−45 degrees F) is native to the eastern United States; its pads are bright green and its flowers vivid yellow. Similarly widespread but found instead in the West is *Opuntia polyacantha* (plains prickly pear, hardy to −25 degrees F). *Opuntia fragilis* (to −35 degrees F) grows throughout Canada and the West into Mexico.

Tropical cacti

It seems a contradiction in terms, but tropical cacti exist. Native to rain forest regions of the world, these prefer high humidity, warmth, and rich soil. In habitat, most are epiphytes ("air plants" that use trees for support but do not derive nourishment from them). Most widely cultivated are those with brilliant, water lily–like blooms.

Epiphyllums (orchid cacti) produce impressive flowers in late spring; named cultivars come in every hot hue. Foliage consists of long, flat, jointed pads with scalloped edges.

Flowers of popular *Schlumbergera truncata*, from Brazil, appear in midwinter, hence the common name Christmas (or holiday) cactus. Pads are flat, jointed, and flexible; flowers white, pink, red, or purple. Keep dry during summer dormancy. *Hatiora* (syn. *Rhipsalidopsis*), commonly called

Opuntia polyacantha (plains prickly pear) is among several Great Plains species that survive temperatures well below zero. Denver Botanic Gardens.

Three different epiphyllums in bloom. Peggy Petitmermet garden, Elfin Forest, CA.

Easter cactus, also is from Brazil; its flowers are similar to those of *Schlum-bergera*, but the stamens do not extend beyond the petals. Leaf margins of Easter cactus are lined with tiny hairs.

Stems of *Rhipsalis* (rope cactus) are long and delicate, and grow densely, making them good filler plants for tall pots, terraces, and hanging baskets. Similar in growth habit is *Lepismium*, a genus likely to surge in popularity as it becomes more available. Particularly showy is *Lepismium cruciforme*, the stems of which turn magenta in summer given adequate light. Plants produce diminutive white flowers followed by beadlike, purple-pink fruit.

Roots of tropical cacti require ample oxygen. Grow them in moss-lined hanging baskets in a light, quick-draining mix of half-and-half perlite and potting soil, or use a bagged orchid mix. Indoors, the perfect environment for the plants is on a shelf beneath a skylight near a steamy shower. Tropical cacti also thrive in hothouses, lath houses, and screened porches. Outdoors, the plants usually are grown in a breezy, open area, beneath latticework or lacy trees.

Tropical cacti bloom best when given a lot of light, provided they are not allowed to sunburn. Cool temperatures and/or long nights also are essential to flowering. In mid-September, encourage dormancy by reducing water and placing the plants where nighttime temperatures stay between 55 and 68 degrees F. Buds should appear in a few weeks. If your home or greenhouse stays warmer than that, limiting the amount of light the plants receive is the next best method; place them where they will receive no light, including artificial, from sunset to sunup.

Keeping plants pot-bound promotes bloom. Prevent bud drop by giving adequate light, not allowing the soil to dry out, and maintaining temperatures above 40 degrees F.

Water tropical cacti, during active growth, daily or as needed to keep soil well moistened. Propagate in summer by taking cuttings, and protect from frost in winter. Feed regularly with a low-nitrogen fertilizer. Boost the phosphorous six months prior to flowering, then cease feeding three months before bloom.

Lepismium cruciforme. R. C. and Beverly Cohen residence, Newport Beach, CA.

Calandrinias

Cistanthe grandiflora (syn. *Calandrinia grandiflora*) forms low-growing clumps of gray-green rosettes that send up thin, airy flower stalks topped with neon purple, poppylike flowers. Grow in masses to enhance the plants' visual impact; give rich soil and regular applications of dilute fertilizer. Calandrinias do best when soil is not allowed to dry completely. A summer grower, it prefers mild, maritime climates where it receives full sun. In winter, it all but disappears.

Cotyledons

Plants in the genus *Cotyledon* are native to Africa. *Cotyledon orbiculata* has thick leaves that are green or gray, and slender or pancake-like. Leaves may be wavy and edged with a thin line of red. Plants send up foot-tall flower stalks in summer topped with tubular, coral, bell-shaped blooms. These attract ants that colonize them with aphids; be vigilant or the flower show will be ruined.

Different from *Cotyledon orbiculata* in appearance is *Cotyledon tomentosa*, which has plump green leaves that vary from grape- to thumb-sized. These are fuzzy and tipped with dark red points, hence the common name kitten paws. *Cotyledon tomentosa* serves as a good filler plant and eventually forms a small shrub. The variegated form is striped with cream.

Crassulas

There are numerous species and cultivars of *Crassula*, and two main forms: jadelike and stacked.

Jades have thick stems and form mounding, branching shrubs that can be pruned into small trees and used for bonsai. Flowers appear midwinter through spring, borne in clusters that may be massed so profusely the plant appears blanketed with snow. Common jade (*Crassula ovata*) has thumb-sized, oval green leaves edged in red. Silver dollar jade (*Crassula arborescens*) has red-edged silvery gray leaves. Sunset jade (*Crassula ovata* 'Hummel's Sunset') turns bright yellow and blushes with orange and red when given adequate sun; in shade, it reverts to green. Two cultivars of *Crassula ovata* with involuted (inward-rolled) tips include 'Hobbit' (leaves resemble sows' ears) and 'Gollum' (leaves are more tubular).

(top left) *Cotyledon orbiculata* grows in the midst of the ornamental grass blue fescue (*Festuca glauca*). David Feix garden, Berkeley, CA.

(top right) Two types of jade share a talavera pot: *Crassula ovata* (with rounded leaves) and its cultivar 'Gollum'. Charlene Bonney garden, Encinitas, CA.

A metal sculpture of a cat holds a terracotta pot filled with an appropriate plant: kitten paws (*Cotyledon tomentosa*). Art and Sandra Baldwin garden. Metal art by Richard Kolb, Yardbirds, Louisville, KY.

Many crassulas intensify in color when stressed. *Crassula perforata* turns rosy purple; *Crassula ovata*, red-orange; and *Crassula nudicaulis* var. *platyphylla*, burgundy. Alice Van de Water garden, Santa Barbara, CA.

Crassula tetragona cuttings resemble trees.

Jades are tough, resilient, unfussy plants with remarkable water storage capabilities and survival skills. They also may prune themselves—limbs soften, shrivel, and fall off, resulting in a balanced shrub and fallen branches that root readily.

Crassula sarcocaulis (bonsai crassula) has a gnarled trunk with peeling bark; it forms a small (2-foot) branching shrub. Flowers are pale pink. It is one of the hardiest crassulas, tolerating temperatures down to 10 degrees F.

Useful in miniature landscapes because it resembles a pine tree is *Crassula tetragona*, an upright plant with inch-long, pointed green leaves that grow at right angles to the slender stems. *Crassula pubescens* subsp. *radicans* is prized for its tightly clustered, tiny, brilliant red leaves (the more sun, the redder). It has a creeping growth habit and blooms that resemble buds of clover.

(top left) *Crassula perforata.*

(top right) The diameter of these *Crassula capitella* leaves averages about an inch.

Strands of baby's necklace (*Crassula rupestris* subsp. *marnieriana*) turn upward, like eels. Design by Pamela Volante, Pamela Volante Interior Planning and Design, Westwood, CA.

Stacked crassulas have leaves that appear threaded along ever-lengthening, wiry, pendant stems that turn upward as they seek light. Leaves might be long or short; square, triangular, or oval; and loosely or tightly packed. In some cases the older leaves frame newer and smaller ones, resulting in intriguing pyramids of foliage.

The largest stacked crassulas have 6-inch-long leaves; the smallest, $\frac{1}{16}$ of an inch. For hanging baskets in windy areas or likely to be brushed by passersby, stacked crassulas are a better choice than graptopetalums or senecios, because leaves of crassulas do not detach easily.

Flowers of *Crassula perforata* are skinny extensions of the stem and not particularly showy; those of the other main species of stacked crassula, *Crassula rupestris*, are globular pom-poms. *Crassula capitella* has narrow and pointed stacked leaves; longer-leaved *Crassula* 'Campfire' (sometimes identified as *Crassula capitella* 'Campfire') turns orangey red when grown in full sun. *Crassula perfoliata* var. *falcata* (propeller plant) has gray, canoe-shaped leaves and dense clusters of bright red flowers that bloom in summer. Dainty watch-chain crassula (*Crassula muscosa*) resembles green yarn; it is useful in animal topiaries for ears and tails. *Crassula pyramidalis* has four-lobed leaves so tightly stacked that when viewed from the side, it appears herringboned.

Vining crassulas include *Crassula multicava*, which is long and lanky but thrives where most other succulents will not: in full shade. Its method of reproduction is interesting—tiny new plants form on flower stalks as blooms fade. More ornamental and also tolerant of low-light conditions (but uncommon) are *Crassula umbella* (lily pad–like leaves encircle red stems; green-and-pink flowers are borne in clusters) and *Crassula streyi*, which has stiff, oval leaves that are dark green and glossy on top and maroon underneath. Around Christmastime vining crassulas produce tiny white flowers that suggest shooting stars.

Keep winter-blooming crassulas dry during their summer dormancy.

CRESTED SUCCULENTS

Crested growth—which sometimes looks as though the plant's tissues were gathered, like fabric along the waistband of a skirt—is a phenomenon found more in cacti and succulents than the rest of the plant world. Convoluted cacti may suggest brain coral, and leaves of aeoniums and graptopetalums may bunch together so tightly they appear frilled. Like caudiciforms, such mutant succulents can be rare and valuable, especially when large, as they tend to be slow growing.

Fasciation—flattening or fanning of stems—is typical of crested (also called cristate) succulents and falls under the larger category of monstrose (which includes abnormalities such as bumps, beaks, points, odd spine formations, weird leaves, and strange colors).

Crested succulents are especially sensitive to sunburn and overwatering. Grow them in a sheltered area in bright shade—or better yet, in a well-venti-

Haageocereus pseudomelanostele 'Cristata'. Buck Hemenway, Inter-City Cactus and Succulent Show, Los Angeles County Arboretum, Arcadia, CA.

lated greenhouse. To prevent rot, give less water than you would a regular plant of the same species.

If a plant has both crested and normal growth, prune away the latter to direct energy to the crest. Otherwise, the more vigorous tissue eventually will take over.

Crests of *Myrtillocactus geometrizans* at left suggest plumes of smoke. Al Richter garden, Glendora, CA.

Dasylirion wheeleri (desert spoon). Al Richter garden.

Dasylirions

Dasylirions, from the desert Southwest and Mexico, consist of lines; like *Agave geminiflora* and *Yucca rostrata*, they form large, spherical pincushions. Few plants are so visually dynamic—dasylirions appear to explode out of their pots. These tough plants do well in containers, providing they get adequate sun and heat.

Dracaenas

Dragon tree (*Dracaena draco*), which has stout branches tipped with clusters of swordlike leaves, eventually gets immense (to 30 feet tall) in the ground but will grow slowly in a pot for years. Dragon trees do not make good houseplants; a better choice is lesser-known *Dracaena arborea*, which is similar but smaller and stays compact and unbranched.

Skinny-trunked *Dracaena marginata* does well indoors or out (if given adequate light); it has long, narrow, leathery leaves. Cultivar 'Tricolor' is striped gold, green, and red—a beautiful plant, especially when backlit.

Dudleyas

Dudleyas, native to the American West and Mexico, include cliff dwellers suitable for tucking into the niches of rock walls. Powdery white leaves make these plants standouts, but avoid touching them as they are easily marred by finger marks. Dudleyas are summer-dormant winter growers that require fresh air, exceptionally well-drained soil, and *no* summer water—even though they may appear drought stressed because their outer leaves dry and curl inward. Red-tipped, silvery leaves of *Dudleya edulis* are shaped like French fries. *Dudleya brittonii*, the most common in cultivation, resembles a chalky gray echeveria.

Echeverias

Echeverias are native to Texas, Mexico, and Central and South America. Appropriately, their colors are as red as salsa, as opalescent as a south-of-the-border sunset, and as blue as the Sea of Cortez. The rosettes resemble water lilies, ruffled lettuce, or camellias. In spring and summer, these send forth bloom spikes a foot long or longer, about the diameter of a pencil, that curl like question marks. If two touch where they curve inward, they outline a heart. Blooms along an echeveria's flower stalk may be cream, yellow, orange, red, pastel pink, or combinations thereof. Some look like candy corn.

Echeverias are not as cold hardy as sempervivums, which they resemble, but they seem to tolerate frost better than many succulents. In my garden, crassulas, euphorbias, and aeoniums were damaged at 25 degrees F, but the echeverias came through fine. Tomentose (fuzzy) echeverias are the most cold tolerant. An example is *Echeveria pulvinata*, which forms a low-growing, branching shrub of blue-green, red-tipped, irregular rosettes. Cultivar 'Frosty' is snowy white. Even hairier, and with a more compact growth habit, is *Echeveria setosa*. *Echeveria* 'Doris Taylor' is a cross between the two species; it has fat, pointed, velvety leaves that form compact rosettes on low stems. Additional cultivars are *Echeveria* 'Pulv-Oliver' and *Echeveria* 'Set-Oliver'.

Hen-and-chickens echeverias (such as *Echeveria imbricata*) form ever-enlarging clumps of offsets that can be wiggled loose and rooted. Pale gray-blue *Echeveria runyonii* 'Topsy Turvy' also offsets freely; its guttered, light gray leaves curve upward and then point down toward the center of the rosette. *Echeveria agavoides* is glossy and looks like a small, fat agave; cultivar 'Lipstick' is bright green with pointed red tips. Similar in form is *Echeveria affinis* 'Black Prince', which is an intriguing reddish brown. But because

A *Dudleya brittonii* rosette is about the size of a bowling ball. Rancho La Puerta, Tecate, Baja California, Mexico.

Echeveria colorata 'Brandtii'.
California Cactus Center nursery, Pasadena, CA.

of its dark color, it presents the same design challenges as near-black *Aeonium arboreum* 'Zwartkop'—it can appear to be a shadowy gap.

Echeveria subrigida, with rosettes of smooth, tapered blue-green leaves margined in red, grows to 2 feet in diameter and as high over time. 'Wavy' is lighter in color; leaves have rippled edges. Beautiful when backlit, its slightly translucent, blue-green leaves have red edges that glow neon bright.

Sedeveria are bigeneric hybrids of echeverias and sedums. Cultivar 'Green Rose' produces sprays of yellow flowers; rosettes are symmetrical clusters.

(next page top left) Echeveria cultivars with ruffled leaves are among the showiest of succulents. Cedros Gardens nursery, Solana Beach, CA. Design by Mia McCarville.

(next page top right) Rosettes of *Echeveria secunda* are effective repeated. These are just beginning to bloom. Nan Raymond residence, Timaru, South Island, New Zealand. Photo by Charles Mann.

(next page bottom) *Echeveria subrigida*. Succulent Gardens nursery.

(left) *Euphorbia tirucalli* 'Sticks on Fire'. Art and Sandra Baldwin garden.

(right) *Euphorbia esculenta* is a medusoid euphorbia.

Euphorbias

The genus *Euphorbia* is immense and by no means limited to succulents—poinsettias, for example, are included.

Succulent euphorbias are sometimes confused with cacti. Tall, branching *Euphorbia ingens* resembles plants in the genus *Cereus*; spherical *Euphorbia obesa*, which grows to about the size of a tennis ball, suggests an astrophytum; and thorns that line the edges of *Euphorbia grandicornis* make the plant as menacing as any cholla. But most cacti have clear, watery sap; that of euphorbias is milky. Spines of cacti radiate from a central point (aureole), which euphorbias lack. Cacti are New World plants; most cactuslike euphorbias come from Africa. And euphorbia blooms are small and beadlike—very different from the vivid-hued, satin-petalled flowers of cacti.

Euphorbia tirucalli 'Sticks on Fire' turns bright orange when stressed. It forms a thicket of loosely branching, vertical stems, each about the diameter of a pencil, that lack prominent leaves. Use the plant to lend color and height to compositions, to resemble an autumn-hued tree in miniature landscapes, and to suggest coral in succulent seascapes. Similar in form is *Pedilanthus macrocarpus* (lady's slipper, so named for the shape of its flowers), a good succulent for desert areas.

Euphorbia milii (crown of thorns) has spiny branches tipped with sprays of dime-sized bracts (leaf clusters that look like flowers) that resemble, from a distance, geraniums. Bracts of this useful shrub—which is seldom out of

(left) The open branching structure of this *Euphorbia milii* (crown of thorns) echoes the lines of the seagull sculpture behind it. Lynn Woodbury Landscape Design, Santa Barbara, CA.

(right) *Euphorbia trigona* 'Rubra'. Cactus Ranch nursery, Reseda, CA.

Though common in cultivation, *Euphorbia obesa* is endangered in its native habitat. California Cactus Center nursery.

bloom—come in all warm colors, including red, yellow, coral, and cream. Dwarf cultivars are ideal for potted arrangements and include those so floriferous that at first glance you might think they are hydrangeas. *Euphorbia milii* 'Dwarf Apache' is one example; it has a compact growth habit and rose red bracts.

Round containers and urns are excellent for framing medusoid (snakelike, named after Medusa in Greek mythology) euphorbias—those that form pinwheels of fleshy, scaly stems. Among them are *Euphorbia esculenta* and *Euphorbia inermis*, which have radiating arms that resemble nubby green sausages; and the more serpentine *Euphorbia woodii*, *Euphorbia flanaganii*, and (appropriately named) *Euphorbia caput-medusae*.

Wear gloves—ideally, disposable ones—when pruning or taking cuttings from euphorbias. You may want to wear eye protection as well. In late spring, when the plants are turgid, their caustic latex may squirt when limbs are cut. Spread newspaper to protect flooring, hardscape, or countertops from drips. To stop the flow, dip cuttings in cold water.

Keep euphorbias, especially those that are cactuslike, on the dry side during winter dormancy. Avoid letting soil dry out during the growing season (midspring through midsummer).

Faucarias

Faucarias form rosettes of fat, wedge-shaped leaves that may be bumpy (*Faucaria tuberculosa*) or have threadlike extensions from leaf margins that make them resemble snapping jaws (*Faucaria tigrina*). They do well as windowsill plants, do not grow unmanageably fast or large, and produce shimmering, ice plant flowers. Keep on the dry side, especially during summer dormancy. Provide plenty of light from late summer through midwinter to encourage bloom.

Gasterias

Gasteria is a genus of thick-skinned succulents that thrive in bright shade. Gasterias have stiff leaves tightly stacked atop each other. The name comes from slender flower spikes lined with what look like little pink stomachs. I find gasteria stalks—and the similar whiplike ones of haworthias—messy, so I snip them off close to the rosette.

The bigeneric cross between *Gasteria* and *Haworthia* is ×*Gasterhaworthia*; cultivar 'Banded Pearls' is dark green with raised white dots loosely arranged in ridges.

Gasterias on display at the Inter-City Cactus and Succulent Show.

Faucaria tigrina in a handpainted talavera pot. The Plant Man nursery. Design by Joyce Buckner.

GRAFTED SUCCULENTS

Grafting involves slicing into a healthy succulent to attach another so that their vascular systems align. The technique is useful in order to propagate or to grow more easily succulents that are crested or variegated. Being attached to a vigorous rootstock makes survival possible for succulents that lack the necessary chlorophyll for photosynthesis.

Spherical *Gymnocalycium mihanovichii* (commonly called moon cactus or hotheads) is an example; because of its neon-bright novelty, it often is a person's first potted plant. I like moon cacti best in multiples, positioned so they lean toward each other as though shuffling to a Latin rhythm. Moon cacti make good windowsill plants, providing they are protected from sunburn—like all grafted cacti, they scorch quickly. Grafted succulents are also highly sensitive to overwatering.

Variegated and crested *Euphorbia lactea*, which looks like melting ice cream, is a popular subject for grafting; prized specimens are intricately convoluted and blend creamy white with shades of green and pink.

(top) An assortment of variegated and crested *Euphorbia lactea*. Collection of Wanda Mallen, Fallbrook, CA.

(bottom) These moon cacti (*Gymnocalycium mihanovichii*) have been grafted onto chlorophyll-rich hylocereus. The Plant Man nursery. Design by Joyce Buckner.

The large rosettes are ×*Graptoveria* 'Fred Ives'; the smaller (in the center), *Graptopetalum paraguayense*. Seaside Gardens.

Graptopetalums

Graptopetalums work well as cascaders, providing they are sheltered from wind and passersby. Their leaves fall off readily, which is one way the plant reproduces; roots form at the stem end.

Graptopetalum paraguayense rosettes resemble those of many echeverias but grow at the tips of ever-lengthening stems. Plants turn pinkish yellow in hot, dry conditions and blue-gray when pampered with partial shade and regular water. Less common is *Graptopetalum pentandrum* subsp. *superbum*, which has compact rosettes of pointed, oval, lavender leaves.

Bigeneric hybrids of *Echeveria* and *Graptopetalum* are ×*Graptoveria*, and among these is 'Fred Ives', which forms large (to 6 inches in diameter) rosettes that, depending on the amount of light, blend shades of blue, gray, rose, or yellow. Graptoverias look especially good in pots with a metallic or iridescent sheen.

Graptopetalums and graptoverias tolerate temperatures down to the middle to high 20s F. In spring, plants produce sprays of yellow or beige lanternlike flowers on arching stems.

Haworthias

Closely related to gasterias are haworthias, diminutive succulents from South Africa. Although these popular houseplants need less light than most other succulents, for best color and form they should receive as much sun as possible without burning. Depending on the latitude and time of year, they do well on bright windowsills, beneath shade cloth outdoors, in green-houses, and on patios that receive morning sun and afternoon shade. Introduce nursery-grown plants gradually to greater-light conditions; sunburn can happen in a matter of hours.

Venerable specimens that are well tended invariably win blue ribbons at shows. Among the most intriguing are those that have areas of translucent tissue at their tips, that show prominent veining, and that are red or variegated. Haworthias are wonderful succulents to collect and hybridize, a pursuit enjoyed by enthusiasts worldwide.

Haworthia cymbiformis forms fleshy rosettes that are dark green with windowlike tips. *Haworthia truncata*, with its sliced-looking edges, suggests a toppled stack of Fig Newtons. *Haworthia attenuata* and *Haworthia fasciata* have concave, slender, pointed leaves that are banded with white ridges (hence the common name that they share: zebra plant). *Haworthia coarctata* and *Haworthia reinwardtii* consist of columnar rosettes dotted with white tubercles (protuberances on the leaves); the plants blush bronze when grown in bright light (but if they turn orange-red, they are getting too much).

Other popular species include *Haworthia pumila*, which has slender, pointed leaves with white tubercles, which in some cultivars may be doughnut shaped; *Haworthia limifolia*, with washboard ridges and pointed leaves—and those with plump foliage, such as *Haworthia mirabilis* var. *badia* (which has leaves like thick gelatin); *Haworthia comptoniana* (leaves with web-like veining); *Haworthia bayeri* (wedge-shaped leaves, often veined); and *Haworthia magnifica* var. *splendens*, which displays beautiful shades of rose in normal light.

Many haworthias come from regions with almost no summer rain; reduce water during that season but do not allow the soil to dry out completely. Fertilize lightly with spring and fall waterings. Repot haworthias when they begin to crowd their pots, or after two to four years if salts have accumulated in the soil.

Use spiky-leaved haworthias that resemble agaves or aloes in miniature landscapes to suggest the larger succulents.

Haworthia pumila may produce offshoots along its bloom stalks. Collection of Bob Kent, Poway, CA.

Variegated *Haworthia cymbiformis*. The Plant Man nursery.

In February, ruschia is beginning to bloom as purple fountain grass (*Pennisetum setaceum* 'Rubrum') is ending. Shady Canyon, Irvine, CA.

ICE PLANTS

When grown as ground covers, ice plants form dense, ever-spreading mats and produce vivid-hued, dime-sized, daisylike blooms in spring or summer. These attributes also make them ideal for hanging baskets, window boxes, and terraces—any container that would benefit from vigorous growers that cascade. Although good fillers, ice plants are showy only when in flower. Their blooms open in sun and close in dim light.

Red apple ice plant (*Aptenia cordifolia*), which has bright green leaves and red flowers, is a ubiquitous ground cover in the Southwest. It seldom is grown as a potted plant but can serve as a lovely addition to wreaths and hanging baskets. A white-edged variegate is beautiful when contrasted with dark green foliage. Because of red apple's tendency to become rangy, pinch stems back to encourage fullness.

Delospermas from the high mountains of South Africa are renowned for their hardiness. *Delosperma cooperi* (to –15 degrees F) has dark green leaves and purple flowers; the flowers of *Delosperma* 'Kelaidis' (also known as *Delosperma* 'Mesa Verde', to –25 degrees F) are salmon pink. Blooms of *Delosperma nubigenum* (to –15 degrees F) are yellow; when stressed, its leaves blush red.

Drosanthemum floribundum (rosea ice plant) and shrub-forming *Drosanthemum hispidum* have purple-pink flowers that appear in carpetlike profusion. Both are hardy to the mid-20s F.

The genus *Ruschia* (formerly *Lampranthus* and *Oscularia*) has brilliant blooms; those of *Ruschia aureus* are yellow-orange. Excellent in pots and hanging baskets is *Ruschia deltoides*, which has blue-green leaves, dark red stems, and pink-purple flowers. Plants tolerate temperatures into the low 20s F for brief periods.

Plants in the genus *Glottiphyllum* have juicy, thin-skinned leaves that are long and tonguelike. Glottiphyllums do well in containers but are easily damaged.

Hesperaloes

Though not a yucca, *Hesperaloe parviflora* is commonly called Texas red yucca and indeed is widely cultivated throughout the Lone Star State. This heat lover, native to central Texas, northern Mexico, and the Chihuahuan desert, forms clumps of slender, upright, arching leaves that are blue-green and thornless. In summer, from the centers of the shrubs (which grow to 3 feet tall over time) rise tall stems lined with rosy red, bell-shaped blooms. A highly desirable yellow-flowered form exists. *Hesperaloe parviflora* thrives in temperatures above 100 degrees F (in fact, requires them for best bloom), is hardy to −20 degrees F, and does well in containers.

Kalanchoes

Shapes and textures of kalanchoe (pronounced "kah-lan-KOH-ee") leaves range from smooth, green, and glossy to nubby, gray, and jagged. Flowers vary from clusters of tiny stars to bean-sized bells on multibranched stalks. In habitat, the plants are found from South Africa to Vietnam, along the tropical portions of the world. They are relatively new to cultivation, having been introduced to the nursery trade during the latter half of the 20th century.

Kalanchoes are frost tender, but those with established roots may regenerate after the plant dies to the ground. In my garden, after near-record low temperatures (to 19 degrees F), paddlelike leaves of *Kalanchoe luciae* collapsed like wet Kleenex. In spring, florets of new leaves encircled the bases of the old, dead stalks. Commonly called flapjack plant, *Kalanchoe luciae* has teal-colored leaves tipped in red (the more sun or cold, the redder). The plant is prized for its foliage, but the way it flowers is also intriguing; the center of the plant elongates into a minaret.

A widely sold and popular houseplant is *Kalanchoe blossfeldiana* (supermarket kalanchoe). Plants have shiny, dark green leaves with scalloped edges and produce masses of dainty flowers in an assortment of candy hues. Retailers do the plants a disservice by encasing the pots in foil sleeves that allow water to puddle—these should be removed soon after purchase.

Kalanchoe beharensis (Napoleon's hat) forms a diminutive tree that over time grows to about 10 feet tall (in the ground). Arching, gray-green leaves are large, stiff, and felt-textured. Do not place in a windy area, lest limbs break; even in a protected corner, the gnarled trunk may need staking.

(left) *Kalanchoe luciae.* Don and Jill Young garden, San Diego, CA.

(right) *Kalanchoe beharensis.*

Kalanchoe blossfeldiana. Chicweed, Solana Beach, CA.

Two kinds of *Kalanchoe tomentosa* (the species and 'Golden Boy') share a pot with teal echeverias. Courtyard Pottery, Solana Beach, CA.

Kalanchoe orgyalis. Claire and Jerry Parent garden, Santa Barbara, CA. Design by Sydney Baumgartner.

Othonna capensis. Art and Sandra Baldwin garden.

Shrub-forming *Kalanchoe orgyalis* has 4-inch-long oval leaves that are silvery green on one side and fuzzy bronze on the other. Leaves of *Kalanchoe longiflora* var. *coccinea* (syn. *Kalanchoe petitiana*) are spoon-shaped and scalloped, and turn crimson when the plant receives full sun. Thumb-sized leaves of low-growing and spreading *Kalanchoe pumila* are blue-gray and covered with fine white powder; the flowers are bright pink. *Kalanchoe tomentosa* (panda plant) has stiff, fuzzy leaves. Those of *Kalanchoe marmorata* (penwiper plant) range in color from beige to teal and are speckled.

A subcategory of *Kalanchoe* once classified as a separate genus is *Bryophyllum*. These produce plantlets that grow along leaf margins, hence a name that applies to more than one species: mother of thousands. When mature, plantlets detach easily and root readily—so much so, they can pop up like weeds. They redeem themselves by producing parasol-like clusters of pendant red-orange flowers atop tall stems.

Lewisias

Lewisias, North American natives named after explorer Meriwether Lewis, are hardy to around −20 degrees F. New and colorful kinds of *Lewisia cotyledon*, with clarkia-like flowers that range from shades of orange through rosy pink and purple, are gaining popularity and becoming widely available. Cultivars produce a stronger, longer-lasting flower show and are less temperamental about being overwatered. Once considered rare is *Lewisia tweedyi*, which has apricot-hued blooms.

Othonnas

Othonna capensis looks like a green version of *Senecio serpens*, but leaves (which average about 3 inches long) are more slender. Flowers—which close in low light—also are senecio-like, in that they are daisy-shaped and persist after blooming as little white puffs (which are not particularly attractive; they look like dandelions). *Othonna capensis* serves as a fast-growing ground cover or cascader that fills in quickly and blooms almost continually, taking a break during summer dormancy. The plant is reputedly hardy to 0 degrees F and possibly lower. In growth habit and cultivation requirements, it is similar to *Delosperma* and also is from South Africa.

LIVING STONES

Succulents that resemble rocks and pebbles are fascinating but can be challenging to grow. Whenever living stones are mentioned among collectors of cacti and succulents, invariably someone will laugh and say, "I've killed those!" Genera include *Argyroderma*, *Conophytum*, *Fenestraria*, *Lithops*, *Opthalmophyllum*, and *Pleiospilos*. Plants typically consist of smooth-sided, toe-sized leaves, often with windows or dots of translucent tissue that enable photosynthesis.

In their habitat, living stones are nearly buried in mineral-based soils poor in organic matter. The plants receive only a few inches of rainfall a year, so watering—or rather not watering them—is crucial. Living stones rot quickly when overwatered or watered at the wrong time of the year. Plants may split when engorged; one warning sign (which may come too late) is bloating.

If you are wary of living stones because their cultivation seems difficult, let me assure you that it is possible to grow them with great success (although I have killed a few myself, and two on the patio at present seem peaked). As with any finicky plant—rosebushes come to mind—if you do not know what you are doing, disaster may ensue, but once you become knowledgeable, cultivation is easy though nonetheless subject to debate among enthusiasts.

Argyroderma patens (blue pebbles) from South Africa has rounded, paired leaves and is delightful when staged with the smooth stones it resembles. The plants are more forgiving than lithops of excess water (though it should be rarely given in summer) and thrive in light winter rains in temperate climates. Flowers, which occur in late autumn or winter, are bright purple or magenta-pink.

Steven Hammer, a world-renowned authority on lithops in Vista, CA, receives emails daily from people who wonder how much and when to water their plants. Hammer says gardeners can get hung up on soil formulas and watering schedules, which is unfor-

A rock-and-pebble topdressing mirrors the shape and color of argyrodermas. The succulents are split down the middle. Grow nursery, Cambria, CA. Photo and design by Nick Wilkinson. Pot by Tex Buckner.

Flat tops of *Lithops lesliei* 'Albinica' suggest cells undergoing mitosis. Design by Diane Dunhill, Santa Barbara, CA.

Steven Hammer collects pollen from a lithops flower.

tunate because lithops are supremely easy to maintain. "The secret is to observe them," he says, "which, by the way, is not a chore but a pleasure."

Thousands of plants in Hammer's greenhouses reside in 4- or 6-inch-square plastic pots. Many hunker in a coarse potting medium with just their tops showing. Surprisingly firm to the touch, they resemble single- or double-headed buttons with a fissure down the middle.

Hammer advises that the type of pot does not matter, but if you are concerned about overwatering, clay will keep them drier. Too little light causes lithops to elongate; give them four or five hours of full sun daily, ideally in the morning. Protect from harsh afternoon and summer sun. If your new plants have been in a greenhouse, introduce them to sun gradually so they do not burn; Hammer recommends draping them with a paper napkin for several days.

Leave lithops alone from late fall through spring. Around November, the plant body will open to produce a new pair of leaves. As these grow, they feed off the old leaves, which gradually shrivel and become papery. In winter, protect lithops from frost. Begin watering in spring, once absorption of old leaves is complete. Through summer, observe the plants and water only if wrinkles appear for several days. (Late afternoon stress wrinkles do not count.) Let water drench the roots and flow out of the bottom of the pot.

Most of all, enjoy them. In summer, watch for shimmering flowers to appear. "Be sure to sniff them," Hammer advises. "They're sweet scented."

Euphorbia stellata, with its caudex elevated. Inter-City Cactus and Succulent Show. Design by Matthew Brown and Diane Suzuki.

PACHYFORMS

Rather than relying on foliage to sustain them during dry spells, pachyform succulents draw on built-in water storage tanks. These might be symmetrical or irregular; spherical, oblong or bottle-shaped; smooth or gnarled; and green, brown, or gray. A few have papery, peeling skin; others, hard shells. Leaves of many pachyforms are delicate and disappear during dormancy.

Pachyforms with a caudex (a bulbous stem or root) are caudiciforms; those that are treelike, with fat trunks and/or limbs, are pachycauls (and are described as pachycaulescent).

As evidenced at cactus and succulent shows, pachyforms are a popular subject for bonsai, and collectors enjoy staging the plants to show off their potato-like stems or roots. It can take years for pachyforms to amount to much, and large specimens tend to be expensive. Rare, mature, field-collected plants can be extremely difficult to cultivate and are protected by international law that prohibits trade in endangered species. But many wonderful pachyforms are being cultivated by small-scale commercial greenhouses and backyard hobbyists. These plants have adapted to and thrive in a "captive" environment, and many are far faster growers than they at first appear to be.

Pachyform and pachycaulescent succulents include:

Beaucarnea recurvata. Christi and Richard Reed residence, Georgetown, CO.

A cussonia's leaves resemble snowflakes. Diane Dunhill garden.

Adenia glauca. This pachyform has a large, irregularly spherical, dark green caudex that in its native habitat (arid East Africa) can attain upwards of 2 feet in diameter. From this grow vining stems that produce pale green leaves and chartreuse flowers.

Adenium obesum. These pachycaulescent trees have funnel-shaped blooms that resemble oleanders. Flowers range from cream and white through shades of purple and red, and bicolors also exist. Glossy dark green leaves are about 6 inches long. Take care when pruning; the milky sap is toxic.

Beaucarnea recurvata (bottle palm). This pachyform grows into a tree that resembles a mop atop a suction cup. *Beaucarnea stricta* has straight leaves that radiate like a Fourth of July sparkler.

Burseras. These semiwoody succulent shrubs come from arid regions of Latin America and the desert Southwest. *Bursera microphylla* (elephant tree) has a light gray trunk; that of *Bursera hindsiana* (copal) is reddish. Both have tiny leaves.

Cussonia. This little-known genus of pachycaulescent South African trees has leaves that grow toward the ends of the branches, in clusters. Of the ten species, *Cussonia paniculata* and *Cussonia spicata* are most common in cultivation.

A rare, trophy-winning *Cyphostemma bainesii* (syn. *Cypho-stemma seitziana*). Inter-City Cactus and Succulent Show. Design by Larry Grammer.

The irregular shape of a *Fockea edulis* caudex adds to its appeal. California Cactus Center nursery. Design by Larry Grammer. Pot by Charles Ball.

Cyphostemmas (wild grape). These tree-forming succulents from Africa and Asia have fat, lumpy trunks and taco-shaped leaves with serrated edges. Sprays of unimpressive flowers give way to clusters of beautiful-but-poisonous red-orange, marble-sized berries.

Dioscorea elephantipes (turtleback plant). The hard, semispherical caudex consists of polygons and resembles a tortoise's shell. From this emerge, during the growth season, three or four finger-thick stems that sprout dark green leaves. From the Eastern Cape of South Africa.

Ficus palmeri. This member of the fig family, native to Baja California, has dark green, heart-shaped leaves with red midribs and veins. Roots of young trees are shaped like yams and over time become convoluted. Young *Ficus palmeri* is fast growing and therefore good for the impatient hobbyist.

Fockea edulis. Out of what looks like scaly white sausages rises a slender trunk that branches every which way; leaves are small, oval, and bright green. A good plant for beginners, *Fockea edulis* is a relatively fast grower that is not overly sensitive to cold, is resilient if over- or underwatered, produces pleasing little flowers in late summer, and is pest resistant. Prune to keep compact.

Jatropha cathartica has a moonlike caudex.

An 18-year-old bonsai'd *Operculicarya decaryi.* Design by Rudy Lime, San Diego, CA.

Jatropha cathartica (syn. *Jatropha berlandieri*). This genus in the *Euphorbia* family has a similarly milky, toxic sap. Masses of small, bright red flowers appear on long stems; gray-green leaves are deeply lobed.

Operculicarya decaryi (Madagascar bonsai). Dark, rice-sized, glossy leaves cluster along flexible branches that are easily shaped with wire, in the tradition of bonsai. Prefers moister conditions than most succulents (except during dormancy) and has tuberous roots that can be elevated.

Pachypodiums. Silvery, prickly branches of pachypodiums end in bunches of bright green, oval leaves. Large, fragrant, plumeria-like flowers are followed by ornamental seedpods. *Pachypodium lamerei* (Madagascar palm), the most common species, does well in pots and grows into a small tree. *Pachypodium lealii* subsp. *saundersii* has a broad, bulbous base from which multiple trunks sprout. *Pachypodium geayi* is tall and slender with narrow, lancelike leaves. Fat, globular stems of *Pachypodium brevicaule* suggest prickly eggs.

Pachypodium brevicaule. California Cactus Center nursery.

Uncarinas. These multibranched, pachycaulescent trees from Madagascar have fuzzy, sticky green leaves and showy summer blooms that are yellow or pink with dark throats. Flowers are followed by flat, pointed seedpods (hence the common name, unicorn tree) that are covered with barbed hooks. Remove the pods when they are still green and pliable (if they are dry, use long-handled clippers or hemostats) and dispose of carefully. Uncarinas make beautiful bonsai, and their roots can be elevated.

This *Uncarina grandidieri* specimen started as a cutting nine years earlier. Orange Coast College, Costa Mesa, CA. Design by Joe Stead.

Pachyphytum oviferum.

Pachyphytums

Pachyphytums (the name means thick-leaved—literally, elephantine) are slow-growing succulents with plump, oval leaves that resemble Jordan almonds. Similar to graptopetalums, pachyphytum rosettes form on ever-lengthening stems. Handle gently; leaves pop off readily, and stems can become denuded. Set detached leaves atop coarse potting medium; as it drains the mother leaf, a new plant will form. Leaves' pearlescent, powdery coating rubs off easily—take care lest you leave fingerprint blotches. Plants are hardy to the mid-20s F, but prefer 40 to 80 degrees F.

Bigeneric hybrids of *Pachyphytum* and *Echeveria* (×*Pachyveria*) look like plump echeverias.

Portulacas

Often grown from seed, portulaca (rose moss) is a popular annual for sunny borders and window boxes. The spreading plants, which bloom brightly in shades of pink, orange, and yellow, also do well in hanging baskets. Double-flowered strains of *Portulaca grandiflora* include 'Magic Carpet' and 'Sunkiss'.

(top left) *Portulacaria afra* 'Variegata'. California Cactus Center nursery.

(top right) *Sansevieria cylindrica* consists of a fan of stiff, cylindrical leaves. California Cactus Center nursery.

Portulacarias

Portulacaria afra (elephant's food) sometimes is confused with *Crassula ovata* (jade plant) because the plants look alike, but portulacaria leaves are smaller and the stems are wiry—in fact, are difficult to sever without clippers or a knife. Plants are tough and malleable, easily handle drastic pruning, and make good bonsai subjects. *Portulacaria afra* is green with red stems and grows into a large shrub; a dwarf, pendant form is available. *Portulacaria afra* 'Variegata' has a prostrate growth habit and yellow-variegated leaves. When drought stressed and given full sun, portulacaria produces sprays of tiny purple blooms.

Sansevierias

Sansevierias make excellent houseplants, as they tolerate dim light, require minimal water, and like the same temperatures humans do. With their vertical, tapered, and rigid leaves, the plants give intriguing linear shapes and vertical interest to container compositions. The simple silhouette of sansevierias lends elegance to any setting and is especially suited to contemporary interiors.

(above) *Sedum nussbaumerianum.* R. C. and Beverly Cohen garden.

(left) *Sansevieria trifasciata* 'Laurentii' undulates upward from its container. R. C. and Beverly Cohen residence.

Sansevierias are unfussy about soil. The key to keeping them healthy is to water them regularly during warm months and very little during cool. The plants spread via underground rhizomes that will crowd a pot to the point that it may crack and break. If roots are thickly massed, use a hacksaw to divide them.

It is a misconception that sansevierias are highly toxic; even so, do not place one where a pet or toddler might chew it.

Sedums

Long grown as ground covers and rock garden plants, sedums (stonecrop) recently have become popular for green roofs (verdant, ecologically sensible rooftop gardens).

Leaves of trailing sedums range from smaller than a grain of rice to as big as bullets. *Sedum nussbaumerianum*, one of the larger-leaved, turns bright yellow when grown in full sun. *Sedum rubrotinctum*, which reddens when

(top left) *Sedum spathulifolium* 'Cape Blanco' in bloom. Cambria Shores Inn, Cambria, CA.

(top right) *Sedum burrito*. Design by Pamela Volante.

(bottom) *Sedum makinoi* 'Ogon' is good for brightening shady areas.

stressed, has the misleading common name pork and beans—leaves more closely resemble jelly beans. Cultivar 'Aurora' is pink.

Blue-green *Sedum morganianum* (donkey tail) forms thick, ropy strands. Stems will grow quite long—4 feet or more. When brushed against or handled, leaves fall off, so donkey tail is not the best choice for arrangements that need to be repotted frequently or are in high traffic areas. Plant in a container with a rolled rim; one that is thin will shear leaves from stems. The bullet-shaped leaves of *Sedum morganianum* are larger and lighter in color than those of its counterpart *Sedum burrito* (burro tail), which has shorter, blunter, and more densely packed leaves. These are bluish-green, do not fall off as readily, and grow in tightly clustered spirals. Because of its ability to withstand rougher handling, burro tail is the one most often sold in nurseries, but donkey tail is probably more common in gardens worldwide—not only does it propagate readily (one leaf will start a whole new plant), but it also has had a 40-year head start.

Dime-sized, blue-green leaves of *Sedum spathulifolium* resemble diminutive roses or camellias. Cultivar 'Cape Blanco' is silvery gray. *Sedum spurium* (syn. *Phedimus spurius*) 'Dragon's Blood' forms dark red, scalloped rosettes. *Sedum pachyclados* (syn. *Rhodiola pachyclados*) is hardy to −25 degrees F; its lobed leaves are light blue-green and its flowers cream colored.

Sedum palmeri produces masses of large blooms that engulf the foliage. Balconies in Milan and elsewhere in Italy are lined with *Sedum palmeri* in April; when you look up at residential buildings, you see row after row of bright yellow flowers.

Tiny-leaved sedums can visually disappear in a garden but when grown in diminutive pots and displayed so they can be seen close-up, their foliage is enchanting. Dark green leaves of *Sedum anglicum* are rice sized; those of similarly small *Sedum furfuraceum* form tight clusters of blue-green beads that blush pink. Even more dainty is *Sedum dasyphyllum*. *Sedum* 'Blue Spruce' has blue-green, narrow, spiky (but soft) leaves; *Sedum* 'Angelina' resembles 'Blue Spruce' but is bright chartreuse. Golden-yellow *Sedum makinoi* 'Ogon' tolerates shade.

In addition to trailing and creeping sedums, there exist shrub sedums such as large-leaved *Sedum oxypetalum* and those that die to the ground in winter and return in spring. *Sedum* 'Autumn Joy' (to 2 feet tall) produces red-toned, broccoli-like flower heads in fall. More interesting in terms of foliage is *Sedum* 'Purple Emperor', which has burgundy leaves and crimson flowers. A garden standby in England is *Sedum* 'Vera Jamison', which has rose-pink flower clusters and purplish-green foliage.

Sedum 'Angelina' surrounds *Echeveria* 'Afterglow'. Plantplay nursery, Carlsbad, CA.

In this monochromatic composition, blue echeverias and blue *Sedum dasyphyllum* var. *macrophyllum* combine in a blue glazed pot. Greta and Mike Jarvis garden, Manhattan Beach, CA. Design by Sandy Koepke.

Should you run across a succulent that looks like a cross among several rosette-forming genera—*Sedum*, *Echeveria*, and *Sempervivum*, with perhaps a little *Aeonium* thrown in—it is likely *Rosularia*, sometimes considered a subgenus of *Sedum*. These green, mounding plants from Turkey grow in crevices in cliffs and rock walls. Flowers—in pastel hues of pink, yellow, and cream—are pointed stars held aloft on vertical sprays. Rosularias are ideal succulents for cold-climate rock gardens and are becoming more common in nurseries that specialize in alpine plants.

The majority of sedums are frost hardy, and some—such as *Sedum spurium*—go well below zero. Most prefer cool climates and require sun protection, especially in summer. Rather than attempting to take cuttings to propagate a fine-textured sedum, use a trowel to dig up part of a clump and then replant it, soil and all.

Sempervivums

Sempervivums (houseleeks) are sometimes confused with echeverias because plants in both genera are rosette shaped and may form ever-enlarging clumps. But leaves of echeverias are plumper; those of sempervivums are thin and delicately—sometimes almost imperceptibly—fringed. Sempervivums are also better than echeverias at establishing colonies (the main rosette sends out runners).

The numerous species of *Sempervivum* range in color from green and blue-gray through shades of red, and some are bicolored. Mature rosettes vary from matchbox- to softball-sized. Plants in the genus *Jovibarba* are sometimes included in *Sempervivum*; jovibarbas are similar but heftier, and they flower and divide differently. They are very hardy. *Jovibarba* flowers are bell shaped with pale yellow petals.

Rosy pink, starlike sempervivum blooms appear along arching spikes, and then the rosette dies. Not all rosettes in a cluster flower at once, so this is not a great loss. It is pointless to attempt to discourage flowering by pinching out the bloom stalk—as with other monocarpic succulents, the rosette is a goner regardless.

Despite the botanical name, which means "ever living," sempervivums need regular water in order to thrive, especially during periods of active growth. They prefer cold, wet climates; most species can grow outdoors year-round in zones 4 through 7. In dry, hot regions, sempervivums are best cultivated in patio pots, in partial sun to bright shade. I grew white-webbed *Sempervivum arachnoideum* (cobweb houseleek) in my garden's succulent

An assortment of sempervivums includes white-webbed cob-web houseleek (*Sempervivum arachnoideum*) and the cultivars 'Rojin' (red) and 'Jungle Shadows' (green and red). Plantplay nursery.

A cultivar of *Sempervivum tectorum* (hen and chickens).

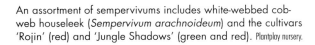

(top) Exuberant sempervivums share a stone trough with dwarf conifer *Pinus mugo* 'Moppet'. Iseli Nursery, Boring, OR. Photo by Randall C. Smith.

Orostachys boehmeri. EuroAmerican Propagators, Bonsall, CA.

tapestry until summer temperatures rose into the 90s F, at which point the plants turned into tight little balls. Before long, they had disappeared (perhaps rolling north to Oregon).

The recommended time to propagate sempervivums is spring; the plants' main growth spurt happens in April and May. Growth slows in the heat of summer, accelerates in autumn, then slows again in winter. To establish sempervivums in a stone wall, pack the crevice with moss, decomposed sod, or fibrous loam and tuck in offsets.

Orostachys is a little-known genus of monocarpic, rosette-forming succulents closely related to *Sempervivum*. Native to Japan and Northern Asia, these cliff dwellers like cool, moist climates and superb drainage. They tolerate temperatures to 0 degrees, and some species are even hardier (*Orostachys spinosa* is unfazed by −40 degrees F). In autumn, the centers of the rosettes elongate to form enchanting pagoda-like blooms.

Senecios

Senecio is an immense genus in the daisy family, but succulent senecios are few, and of those, a mere handful are widely cultivated. One becoming popular with landscape designers in frost-free regions is the ground cover *Senecio mandraliscae* (syn. *Senecio talinoides* subsp. *mandraliscae*), which

String of pearls (*Senecio rowleyanus*) tumbles out of a cast-concrete pot. Also in the composition are sempervivums and echeverias. Design by Molly Wood Garden Design, Costa Mesa, CA.

has light blue, finger-shaped leaves to 4 to 6 inches long. A similar species—that is shorter and therefore a good choice for smaller containers—is the other "blue senecio": *Senecio serpens* (syn. *Senecio repens*).

Bright green *Senecio barbertonicus* (syn, *Senecio talinoides* subsp. *barbertonicus*) a shrub with clusters of long, slender, upthrusting leaves, can add vertical interest to compositions. But because it grows large over time, it may overwhelm other plants. *Senecio amaniensis* has finely haired, silvery green leaves; these are oval and aligned along the upright stems of a loose shrub.

Senecio articulatus (candle plant) is jointed like link sausage and patterned with streaks of red. In winter, a pot of this plant in my home's entryway sends up slender new stems lined with thumbnail-sized, maple-shaped, shiny green leaves. These all face the same direction—sunward, like solar panels, giving the plant an alert look. When guests ask for cuttings, I break off a few cigar-sized pieces (no clippers needed).

Senecio rowleyanus (string of pearls), which has threadlike stems lined with what appear to be peas, suggests dripping water when grown in a dry fountain or birdbath. The plant is, however, finicky when it comes to heat and sun, preferring partial shade and temperatures between 50 and 80 degrees F. Better choices for a sunny location include similarly pendant *Senecio radicans* (string of bananas, which has bean-sized, banana-shaped leaves); *Senecio radicans* 'Fish Hooks', which has crescent leaves; or *Senecio*

herreanus, with leaves the shape and size of gooseberries. Less common are *Senecio jacobsenii*, with flat, overlapping leaves that are shades of greenish pink and maroon, along green stems, and brilliant orange blooms in late summer and early fall; and *Senecio macroglossus*, which resembles ivy but has stiff, waxy, triangular and five-pointed leaves and large (2-inch diameter) pale yellow flowers.

Senecios are grown for the shape and color of their leaves and not for their blooms, which are daisylike and dry into white tufts. The hardiness of senecios, which are summer-dormant winter growers, varies by species; the blue senecios in my garden showed no damage when temperatures dropped to the mid-20s F. Pinch back shrub and creeping senecios to encourage fullness—trim below the topmost pair of leaves and root the cuttings.

Stapelias

Stapelias, from Africa, produce some of the most unusual flowers of any in the plant kingdom; they are star shaped and in color, texture, and scent do their best to resemble decomposing meat. Your dogs may find them fascinating (mine do). The blooms commonly are called carrion flowers; pollinators are flies and beetles. Leaves of most stapelias are soft, four-angled cylinders with ridged edges.

The plants have their main growth spurt in late fall and early winter, which also is when they bloom. They are prone to fungus if allowed to stay damp and cold; keep dry in winter. Stapelias grow well outdoors in the desert Southwest in partial shade. Similar genera (collectively known as stapeliads) include *Hoodia* and *Huernia*, among others.

Synadeniums

Synadeniums are fast-growing succulent shrubs and trees with wine-colored or red-speckled oval leaves. Most of the 20 or so species come from Africa and Madagascar; all have a milky sap that—similar to that of euphorbias—is toxic and irritating to skin and eyes. *Synadenium grantii* and a red-splashed variety are occasionally found in nurseries; they are lovely and deserve wider usage. Synadeniums are excellent for adding height to arrangements and can be pruned to encourage branching. All are highly cold sensitive.

Above trailing green-and-red *Senecio jacobsenii* are the blue fingers of *Senecio mandraliscae*. On their left is *Aeonium* 'Kiwi' and on their right, tucked between them, *Echeveria runyonii* 'Topsy Turvy'. EuroAmerican Propagators.

VINING SUCCULENTS

Grow vining succulents in hanging baskets and in pots atop shelves near sunny windows, or twine the plants around a post, pillar, or trellis. All do best in bright shade.

Rosary vines (*Ceropegia woodii*) suggest a beaded curtain. Half-inch, heart-shaped leaves form pairs at several-inch intervals along thin, flexible stems. Propagate by dividing underground tubers or by collecting those that form on the stems after the plant's odd little flowers fade.

Hoyas (wax flower) come from India, Burma, and China. Stiff leaves—which may be round, oval, or heart shaped—are dark green and sometimes variegated; flowers are nosegaylike clusters in warm colors and appear made of wax.

Less common is *Xerosicyos danguyi* (dollar vine), from Madagascar. This member of the cucumber family has tendrils that aid in climbing. At first glance, perfectly round, flat, 2-inch-diameter leaves appear made of rubber; they are stiff, medium green, and overlap very little. Flowers are insignificant. Fertilize only once during active growth (summer) and keep well above freezing in winter. Propagate from stem cuttings in spring.

Variegated *Ceropegia woodii* (rosary vine). California Cactus Center nursery.

Xerosicyos danguyi. Lotusland, Santa Barbara, CA.

Yuccas

With their slender, spiky leaves, yuccas contrast well with softer-looking succulents and also look good silhouetted against the sky or a wall. Variegates with yellow-and-green-striped leaves are especially beautiful backlit by early morning or late afternoon sun.

Yucca aloifolia (Spanish bayonet) has slender, sometimes prostrate stems tipped with dense, dark green, pointed leaves. *Yucca gloriosa* (Spanish dagger) is similar in appearance but forms multiple trunks; it also tolerates more shade than most yuccas. *Yucca rostrata* has a shimmering topknot of slender leaves. Those of *Yucca baccata* (banana yucca) have fibers along the edges; plants may be stemless or have multiple short stems. *Yucca filamentosa* (Adam's needle) resembles a narrow-leaved agave but has softer foliage; cultivar 'Color Guard' holds its yellow color better than 'Bright Edge'. *Yucca recurvifolia* has a single trunk and soft, downward-curving blue-gray leaves.

Pincushion-shaped yuccas appear interchangeable with agaves and dasylirions that have a similar silhouette, but when a yucca flowers, the differ-

Yucca rostrata lends drama and interest to a pot grouping. Design by Sandy Koepke, Beverly Hills, CA.

Variegated *Yucca filamentosa*. Maggie Judge garden, Encinitas, CA.

ence is obvious; the plumelike inflorescence is massed with creamy white, bell-shaped blooms. Yucca trunks and limbs are lightweight, and cuttings several feet long can be carried in one hand. The wood is corklike; I have sliced through a *Yucca gloriosa* limb several inches thick in seconds using a steak knife. A container needs to be only deep enough to hold the cutting upright, but root formation will be faster the deeper it is planted. Frequent watering and applications of fertilizer will encourage growth; little or none slows it.

Yuccas, which range in habitat from Guatemala to Canada, are unfussy about soil and water, and thrive when pampered. Most species tolerate temperatures below freezing; *Yucca glauca* (soapweed) is exceptionally cold hardy, surviving −35 degrees F. Yuccas are fine in part shade but prefer full sun. Downsides to these easy-to-grow plants are that the base eventually expands into a bulbous mass that can crack or break a container, and that the stiff leaves are sharply pointed.

COMPANION PLANTS

Numerous nonsucculent plants look lovely in combination with succulents and share many of their cultivation requirements. The companions presented here are a few of my favorites, chosen because they offer superb color and texture, are beautiful in their own right, and are used by designers to enhance succulent container gardens, large and small. This is not intended as an exhaustive list but rather an introduction to encourage you to explore creative options offered by genera not classified as succulent.

Companions require more water than succulents but not so much that it will harm those they share containers with. Like succulents, most companions need fast-draining soil, several hours of sun daily in all but hottest climates, and frost protection. If there are exceptions to these requirements, I have noted them.

Bromeliads

Bromeliads are whorled, stemless plants with waxy blooms and pliable yet tough leaves that may be banded, striped, or multicolored. New hybrids are continually being introduced. Bromeliads do best when given high humidity (they appreciate frequent misting) and protection from hot sun (bright

Cryptanthus acaulis, a bromeliad with ribbonlike, pointed leaves, combines well with succulents in floral-style arrangements and wreaths. Island View Nursery, Carpinteria, CA.

Dyckia 'Keswick'. Inter-City Cactus and Succulent Show. Design by Steve Ball.

shade is ideal). For those that have a center cup, give purified water so that it overflows the well and moistens the soil below. The preferred soil mix is one part peat moss and one part bark or perlite. Apply a balanced fertilizer at about half the recommended strength once in spring, twice in summer, once in fall, and not at all in winter.

Dyckias—bromeliads with stiff, sharply serrated leaves—are treacherous but beautifully contrast with soft-leaved succulents and can be used to suggest starfish in undersea-themed arrangements. Colors include green, silvery gray, chocolate brown, and crimson. Similar to dyckias are puyas, which have long, slender, wickedly toothed leaves. Plants in the genus *Hechtia* also are spiny stars; *Hechtia argentea* is a striking silver.

Tillandsia (air plant) is a large genus of epiphytic, tree-dwelling bromeliads, some of which are spiderlike. Many produce brilliant flowers. Tillandsias prefer more humidity than succulents but serve as wonderful accents for wreaths and floral-style arrangements. Those with gray-green and bluish foliage tolerate more sun and have greater drought resistance than tillandsias with green leaves. The plants like to be drenched every few days; if one dries out, soak it to rehydrate.

Cordylines

These foliage plants with slender, upright leaves are sometimes confused with phormiums, but cordylines have an airier growth habit. The plants—which are related to agaves and yuccas, and occasionally are mislabeled as dracaenas—flourish in filtered light and bright shade, and do well indoors. Provide a pot deep enough to accommodate the plant's carrotlike taproot. Named cultivars of *Cordyline australis* make excellent container plants; look for 'Atropurpurea', which has dark purple leaves; 'Red Star' (purplish red); and 'Sundance' (green with a pink midrib). Most are hardy to around 15 degrees F.

Dymondia

I use *Dymondia margaretae* to pave access pathways in my garden's succulent tapestry because succulents cannot be trod upon and dymondia can. This tough, mat-forming ground cover is sold by the flat in nurseries as a landscape plant and seldom is seen in containers. Yet its slender leaves (which are medium green on top and silvery white underneath) look lovely carpeting bare soil in pots and serve as an interesting alternative to sedums and other fillers.

Dwarf conifers

In regions in which sedums and sempervivums thrive year-round, use lovely little evergreen dwarf conifers, which are slow growing and low maintenance, to lend height, color, and texture to arrangements that suggest alpine landscapes. Troughs are traditional for such compositions, but the only requirement is that the container be at least 2 to 3 inches larger all-round than the nursery pot the conifer came in. Genera include *Abies* (fir), *Cedrus* (cedar), *Chamaecyparis* (cypress), *Juniperus* (juniper), *Picea* (spruce), *Pinus* (pine), and *Tsuga* (hemlock). Some dwarf conifers are fluffy or fernlike; others, more bristly. Shapes vary from muffins to spires; foliage, from blue and green to golden yellow. Cones add hues of red. Give dwarf conifers well-drained soil rich in organic matter and keep moist. Protect from temperature extremes and fertilize lightly but regularly.

Epidendrum orchids

The addition of epidendrums (terrestrial orchids) transforms a commonplace potted succulent such as jade into an over-the-top floral arrangement. Epidendrums produce airy stems tipped with pom-pom flower clusters in pink, lavender, red, orange, cream, or yellow. Give these orchids enough sun to flower but not so much that it burns the leaves. Their roots prefer to be cool, and they appreciate regular applications of fertilizer. Deadhead by cutting flower stems back to one or two joints above the soil.

Everlastings (strawflowers)

Papery strawflowers hold their form and hue after they have dried, are crisp to the touch, and remain on the plant—or in a vase, even without water—for months. Sea lavender (*Limonium perezii*) has naturalized along the Southern California coast; it has lush, foot-long leaves and produces cloudlike masses of purple blooms on airy, branching stems, spring through summer. Tiny (⅛-inch) flowers each resemble a paper muffin cup liner, with a white inner part.

The strawflower *Chrysocephalum apiculatum*, an annual formerly in the genus *Helichrysum*, grows to about a foot tall and spreads (in the garden) to 2 or 3 feet wide. Cultivar 'Silver and Gold' has rounded, lance-shaped leaves covered in dense, silvery hairs. Clusters of small, yellow, ball-shaped blooms appear nearly year-round.

Dainty lavender epidendrums repeat the purple-pink of *Echeveria* 'Afterglow'. R. C. and Beverly Cohen garden.

Sea lavender (*Limonium perezii*) grows in combination with *Echeveria agavoides* 'Frank Reinelt' and trailing parrot's beak (*Lotus berthelotii*), a shrubby vine from the Canary Islands. Design by Pamela Volante.

Geraniums (*Pelargonium* spp.)

True succulent pelargoniums exist, but even those classified as nonsucculent tend to be drought tolerant and easy to propagate via cuttings. Excellent in pots, pelargoniums bloom best when their roots are crowded. Use shrub kinds to add height to arrangements; use those that are ivy or scented as fillers and cascaders. Pinch new shoots to promote fullness and deadhead to encourage repeat bloom.

Purple-flowering, scented-leaf pelargoniums spill from a pot that includes a dwarf species with maple-shaped, orange-variegated foliage and salmon flowers. Aeoniums complete the composition. Suzy Schaefer garden, Rancho Santa Fe, CA.

Chrysocephalum apiculatum 'Flambé Yellow' with *Agave americana* 'Marginata'. Quail Botanical Gardens, Encinitas, CA. Design by Katie Pelisek.

Grasses (ornamental)

These feathery plants ripple in the slightest breeze and glow in slanted light. Most ornamental grasses become large over time and should be sheared during dormancy to make way for new growth. Rather than underplanting a vigorous ornamental grass with succulents, give the two separate pots, then juxtapose them in a container grouping. Those mentioned here require less water than most.

Manageably small *Festuca glauca* (blue fescue) is useful for echoing the blue of agaves and contrasts beautifully with their bulk. It is similar to larger, even lovelier blue oat grass (*Helictotrichon sempervirens*), which has tall stems and straw-colored flower clusters. Also silvery blue is California rye grass (*Leymus condensatus* 'Canyon Prince'). *Festuca mairei*, native to Morocco, forms a dense, golden-green mound with gray-green flower spikes. *Pennisetum setaceum* 'Rubrum' (purple fountain grass) has purple foliage and fuzzy arching blooms. *Chondropetalum tectorum* (cape rush) has dark green stems punctuated by bloom spikes tipped with coppery flower heads; after its spring-summer growth spurt it becomes drought tolerant. And *Nassella tenuissima* (Mexican feather grass) is a golden mare's tail, gorgeous planted with purple graptopetalums.

Helichrysums

From South Africa, *Helichrysum petiolare*—which has delicate foliage on long stems that twine through other plants—combines well with succulents in terraces, tall pots, and hanging baskets. Inch-long, licorice-scented leaves are white and woolly; flowers, insignificant. 'Limelight' has bright chartreuse leaves; 'Licorice Splash' is variegated yellow-and-green; 'Variegatum' has white markings.

Nassella tenuissima (syn. *Stipa tenuissima*), commonly known as Mexican feather grass, arches above *Graptopetalum pentandrum* subsp. *superbum* in bud. Design by David Feix.

Helichrysum petiolare 'Variegatum' with *Agave attenuata*. Don and Jill Young garden. Design by Schnetz Landscape, Escondido, CA.

Oxalis spiralis 'Aurea' with *Agave victoriae-reginae* and (in back) *Leucadendron* 'Safari Sunshine'. Flora Grubb Gardens nursery.

Oxalis

Noninvasive, ornamental oxalis is especially appealing in combination with agaves; the oxalis's soft mounds and dainty flowers contrast with the agave's thick, pointed leaves. Red-stemmed *Oxalis spiralis* 'Aurea' (to about 6 inches high) has lime green and gold foliage with coppery highlights; it produces bright yellow flowers that bloom off and on throughout the year.

Phormiums (New Zealand flax)

Phormiums, fan-shaped, clump-forming perennials, are useful as dramatic background plants and to lend height to compositions. For a neat appearance, remove old foliage before new leaves emerge. Phormiums are moderately rapid growers and tough. Leaves will die back during a hard frost, but plants will resprout.

The best known and most common cultivars of *Phormium tenax* typically get so big—6 feet tall and 8 feet wide—that they are unsuitable for all but the largest pots. But dwarfs resulting from crosses of *Phormium tenax* and *Phormium cookianum* are smaller (some as diminutive as 1 foot high at maturity) and have distinctive leaf colors. Those that are dark maroon or brown are striking in combination with red, yellow, or chartreuse-leaved succulents and are beautiful backlit by early morning or late afternoon sun. *Phormium* 'Apricot Queen', to 3 feet high, has slightly arching and twisting, 1-1/2-inch-wide, pale yellow leaves edged in green. 'Maori Maiden', to 2 or 3 feet high, has 1-1/2-inch-wide, apricot to rose red leaves with thin green margins. Foliage color deepens in fall.

Red *Kalanchoe luciae* rosettes ring *Phormium* 'Maori Queen', a variegated dwarf phormium. Hancock Park, Los Angeles, CA. Design by Anna Clark Interiors.

A peach-colored wall serves as a backdrop for a potted garden. *Dracaena marginata*, at right, adds height. Cobalt blue contrasts with the wall and unifies the composition. A few pots are elevated, so the viewer feels surrounded by the garden. Design by Jim Bishop, Bishop Garden Design, San Diego, CA.

Part Three

CREATIVE DESIGNS AND DISPLAYS

This chapter presents out-of-the-ordinary succulent container gardens to enhance your home, indoors and out, plus ideas for effective groupings and placement.

If you have limited space, go vertical; succulents thrive in hanging baskets, planted tubes, wall pots, niches, and wreaths. Tabletop gardens, which include floral-style arrangements, make great gifts. Miniature landscapes that tiny figures stroll, swim, or drive through are fun projects to do with children.

Of particular interest to cactus and succulent collectors are exhibits at juried shows. Judges consider not only a plant's merits, but also the way it is presented, or staged. The award-winning entries shown here represent years—sometimes decades—of meticulous staging and include venerable bonsai.

Succulent specialty nurseries often have someone on staff who makes and refreshes container gardens on a regular basis. Here, too, are descriptions of what a few of these experts are doing, plus examples of their work.

POTS FOR OUTDOOR SPACES

Succulent container gardens can transform bland outdoor spaces into inviting living areas. In turn, the plants benefit from warmth radiated by your home's walls and hardscape, and require little water or upkeep.

Place a potted arrangement near your front door to welcome you home, and for visitors and neighbors to enjoy. Unless among the few kinds (such as sansevierias) that do well in low-light conditions, succulents in sheltered outdoor areas such as entryways need a minimum of several hours of sun daily.

Balconies and rooftops often are excellent habitats for light- and heat-loving succulents, but keep in mind the more exposed the potted garden, the more it will need protection from wind, rain, hail, intense sun, and freezing temperatures. Also make sure pots cannot topple; secure any that are near edges with straps or heavy-gauge wire.

Many trailing succulents, such as *Senecio rowleyanus* (string of pearls) and *Sedum morganianum* (donkey tail), will hang to 4 or 5 feet, provided they are not bumped or buffeted. The longer such plants become, the more impressive, but also the more difficult to move. At the outset, position them where they can remain for years.

A talavera entry pot holds *Sedum burrito* and *Euphorbia milii* (crown of thorns) in bloom. Marilyn Jorgensen garden, Santa Barbara, CA. Design by Rob Lane, Rockrose Garden Design.

Pots alongside a front door are unified by the color red, which is also repeated by red-flowering *Kalanchoe manginii*. The yellow of the wall is echoed by *Aeonium* 'Sunburst', and *Kalanchoe beharensis* fills blank vertical space. Patrick Anderson and Les Olson residence, Fallbrook, CA.

A rooftop garden in New York City combines *Kalanchoe luciae*, a pink-blooming sedum, *Stapelia gigantea*, and annual *Portulaca grandiflora* 'Sundial Yellow'. Design by Ellen Spector Platt. Photo by Alan and Linda Detrick.

Strawberry pots arranged in a curve guide visitors to a home's tiled entry. Design by Jim Bishop.

Sedum morganianum and *sedum burrito* have no difficulty threading through a railing. Karla Bonoff residence, Montecito, CA.

Sedum palmeri in bloom festoons the wrought-iron railing of a tiny balcony worthy of Romeo and Juliet. Vergiano, Italy. Photo by Frank Mitzel.

When grouped on a stepladder, an eclectic assortment of pot-ted succulents becomes a garden focal point. Julie Vanderwilt garden, Santa Barbara, CA.

HOW TO GROUP POTS

An assortment of potted succulents can make a beautiful garden for a patio, deck, or courtyard—especially if you apply basic design principles to the entire grouping.

When deciding how and where to group pots, use any nonnegotiable aspect of the site—such as the color of a wall, flooring, or trim—as your inspiration for contrasting or repeating the kinds of pots you choose. If your patio is surrounded by a hedge, for example, red-glazed pots will stand out against green foliage.

Aim to fill the space so that the effect is just right rather than too much or too little. For example, a half-dozen 2-inch pots in an entryway would seem odd, but those same pots would suit a windowsill. Several 1-gallon pots might be in scale with a patio but would be sparse when spread along a pathway. One way to make too-small pots fit a large space is to cluster and elevate them—perhaps atop a garden bench, shelves, pot stands, overturned pots, bricks, stone slabs, concrete blocks, or even a stepladder.

Pots in a grouping might contain an eclectic assortment of plants, but for continuity, repeat a few throughout—such as sempervivums, Aeonium 'Sunburst', or blue-gray Agave parryi. To enhance the sense of being enveloped in a garden, include tall plants such as beaucarneas, dracaenas, yuccas, Kalanchoe beharensis, or Euphorbia ingens.

Because wet soil is heavy and dampness can be destructive to wood and other porous materials, before you group pots on a deck, balcony, or rooftop, make sure the area can handle their combined weight and is protected from moisture that accumulates beneath them.

(top, left) A cream-colored wall forms the backdrop for pots with milky glazes. In the containers are sedums, echeverias, and a lacy fern. Barbara Baker residence, Rancho Santa Fe, CA.

(top, right) At the Denver Botanic Gardens in summer, tall pots lend height to groupings of colorful containers. Coleus, a nonsucculent annual with frilly green, red, purple, or variegated leaves, lends continuity. Design by Dan Johnson.

(bottom) Terracotta pots, smaller in the foreground and progressively larger, create a patio garden. Mary Rodriguez garden, Rancho Santa Fe, CA.

Pebbles tucked around the inside of the rim of a shallow birdbath help hold in mounded soil. The Water Conservation Garden at Cuyamaca College, El Cajon, CA.

If you have a dry birdbath or fountain, use it to display cascading, rosette, and clump-forming succulents. Moreover, birdbaths, because they are basically a pan atop a pedestal, can be used for miniature landscapes. Consider it a bonus if a leak ruined your fountain or birdbath—it means water will drain.

The top tier of this dry fountain is planted with *Sedum burrito* cuttings, sempervivums, and *Delosperma congestum*; in the lower tier grow *Crassula* 'Campfire', aeoniums, and echeverias. Cottage Gardens nursery of Petaluma and Bennett Valley, CA. Design by Bruce Shanks.

In a blue-glazed birdbath, purple and pink echeveria rosettes suggest water lilies. White-webbed *Sempervivum arachnoideum* rosettes sparkle like sunlight on the surface of water, and in their midst is flat green *Aeonium tabuliforme* (lily pad aeonium). A topdressing of green and blue florists' marbles enhances the illusion. California Cactus Center nursery, Pasadena, CA. Design by Arree Thongthiraj.

(previous page) Forming a fluffy, reddish purple ring around the top tier of this fountain is *Crassula perforata*. Bright green sedum grows in the center top and repeats in the lowest tier, on the left. In the middle tier are more crassulas, green-purple *Senecio jacobsenii*, blue *Senecio mandraliscae*, and yellow-variegated *Aeonium* 'Kiwi'. Silvery blue *Ruschia deltoides* cascades from the lowest tier, and alongside it is green-and-orange *Crassula* 'Campfire'. EuroAmerican Propagators, Bonsall, CA.

If your home's architecture is enhanced by pots atop pedestals, fill the containers with heat- and sun-loving succulents such as agaves and aloes. Fringe these upright plants with trailing graptopetalums, crassulas, sedums, or senecios.

(top) The balcony's blue trim repeats the blue of *Agave colorata*. *Sedum rubrotinctum* adds color and texture. Ken and Deena Altman residence, Escondido, CA.

(left) *Aloe nobilis* provides crisp, upright lines in a composition that includes red *Sedum* 'Dragon's Blood' and *Senecio radicans* 'Fish Hooks'. Shady Canyon, Irvine, CA.

(right) An agave atop an entry pedestal sets the stage for the desert garden beyond. Landscape design by Arcadia Studio, Phoenix, AZ. Photo by Jack Coyier.

Golden-spined rat-tail cactus lends texture and contrasts with graptopetalums that also cascade. Adding height to the composition are fuzzy gray kalanchoes. Also included are *Aloe nobilis* and sempervivums. Timberline Gardens nursery, Arvada, CO. Design by Karen Haataja. Photo by Charles Mann.

KAREN HAATAJA'S DESIGNS

When designer Karen Haataja of Lakewood, Colorado, plants moss-stuffed wire baskets, instead of hanging them she displays them atop a pedestal or overturned pot so succulents in the top can be seen and appreciated.

Haataja, who teaches classes in designing succulent arrangements, credits her degree in fine arts for her compositional skills. Usually, the pot inspires her plant selections. One succulent serves as a focal point, which she positions off center because she considers dead center uninteresting. She repeats colors and textures, lets one element cascade over the edge, and may add rocks or pieces of wood to enhance the overall composition.

Plants in Haataja's tightly packed arrangements settle in well and become established quickly, she says, because she uses slender bamboo sticks as potting tools. Once she positions the plants, she tucks their roots into place with the sticks, which she uses to push the root ball into the soil and, at the same time, to loosen and separate the roots.

(left) A handmade hypertufa pot (center) inspired a composition that includes pieces of wood, kalanchoes, and small cacti and euphorbias. Adjacent containers hold echeverias and sedums. Timberline Gardens nursery. Photo by Randy Tatroe.

(right) Small agaves echo the blue of echeverias and contrast with yellow *Sedum adolphi*, which in turn repeats the color of the bowl. Timberline Gardens nursery. Design by Karen Haataja.

An old bathtub makes a whimsical garden focal point when painted blue and filled with soil and succulents. Cedros Gardens nursery, Solana Beach, CA. Design by Mia McCarville.

(right) When elevated in a teal pot, *Agave desmetiana* 'Variegata' fills blank space in front of a wall. In the foreground, echoing the agave's variegation, is *Aeonium* 'Kiwi'. Whitney Green garden, Santa Monica, CA. Design by Stephen Gabor, Gabor + Allen, Venice, CA.

Whether solo or arranged in multiples, silhouetted against a wall or greenery, large pots lend drama to any setting. Use them to serve as focal points that draw attention away from less desirable areas of the yard, to break up expanses of hardscape, and to provide instant interest to newly planted areas. Large pots give you an opportunity to mass small succulents and/or grow large ones such as agaves, aloes, dracaenas, yuccas, beaucarneas, and dasylirions. And where statuary might seem pretentious, a big container invariably looks good—even when empty.

When choosing a location, keep sight lines in mind. Pathways, fences, walls, and garden beds may individually or collectively point to a logical spot. Also consider areas framed by your home's windows; large pots are useful for creating garden vignettes that enhance views.

Ornamental grasses, yarrow, and wildflowers form a billowy backdrop for a variegated furcraea in a large terracotta pot. Design by Landcraft Environments, Mattituck, NY. Impruneta terracotta pot from Seibert and Rice. Photo by Rob Cardillo.

Pots of succulents and bromeliads serve as an informal barricade along the top of a retaining wall. The pots place the garden at the right height for the owner, who uses a wheelchair. Susan Miller garden, Rancho Santa Fe, CA. Succulent arrangements by Chicweed, Solana Beach, CA. Landscape design by Tom Piergrossi.

(top) A 3-foot-diameter container adds height and interest to a garden bed. Suzy Schaefer garden, Rancho Santa Fe, CA.

Big pots on a slope overflow with pink-blooming *Delosperma* 'Kelaidis'. Positioning them at an angle adds a suggestion of motion and makes their contents more visible and better able to spill. Denver Botanic Gardens. Design by Dan Johnson.

Nolina nelsonii shimmers above two pots; dasylirions, beaucarneas, or yuccas would give a similar effect. The pair of containers are in scale with the fountain, emphasize it as the focal point, connect it with the rest of the garden, and alleviate the expanse of hardscape. San Antonio Botanic Garden, Texas. Photo by Gary Irish.

Rather than stringing pots around a pool's perimeter, group them to suggest a garden. These three hold *Agave lophantha* and *Aloe vera.*
Scott Glenn garden, Santa Barbara, CA.

Succulents are a good choice for pots near pools, fountains, and spas because the plants do not create a lot of leaf litter, have sculptural foliage that is lovely when reflected by water, and thrive in heat radiated by hardscape.

Small agaves underplanted with echeverias in terracotta pots blend the pool area with the yard beyond. San Vincenzo housing development by Pulte Homes, Carlsbad, CA.

A bowl of *Kalanchoe luciae*, geraniums, and senecio sits on a wall alongside a pond. The pot is difficult to access, so low-maintenance plants are ideal. Denver Botanic Gardens.

(top) On either side of a disappearing-edge pool, agaves in pedestal pots are silhouetted against the sky. La Jolla, CA. Design by Rob Ault, Pacific Sun Aquatech, San Diego, CA. Photo by Gary Conaughton.

DISPLAYING YOUR COLLECTION

Invariably when I enter a collector's greenhouse, my initial reaction is that all those lithops or haworthias in pots, lined along shelves, are identical. But as my host introduces me to the plants, I realize how each species or cultivar is unique and fascinating. Collectors savor variations on a theme and have an appreciation for the shapes, textures, and forms of particular types of plants.

To improve your collection's overall appearance, introduce a design element that lends continuity. This might be the color of the pots, the material they are made of, their style and artistry, or their topdressing. If plants are still in their nursery containers, consider repotting them or placing them in cachepots with drain holes. If you are running out of room, go vertical. Shelves arranged like bleachers will effectively display the plants and enable each to receive adequate light.

(top) Shelves on the exterior wall of a garage display an eclectic collection of succulents and decorative objects. Louisa Campagna garden, San Diego, CA. Design by Michael Buckner.

(bottom) A ceramic pan holds small cacti in round pots that contrast with the pan's blue glaze. Vivai Piante Schiavo nursery, Abano Terme, Italy. Photo by Frank Mitzel.

(next page top) Unifying this display of ariocarpus and astrophytums are glazed ceramic pots and a topdressing of crushed rock. California Cactus Center nursery.

(next page bottom) An old soda pop bottle carrier provides a home for cacti and succulents in 2-inch-square pots. Mary Friestedt residence, Del Mar, CA.

What looks like a metal bead is the pivoting joint of a fishing swivel. Suzy Schaefer garden.

A hanging cone has frothy *Sedum spathulifolium* 'Cape Blanco' around the rim. In the center are sempervivums and cuttings of *Crassula* 'Campfire'. Strands of *Senecio rowleyanus* complete the composition. EuroAmerican Propagators. Design by Margee Rader.

To utilize space that otherwise would be wasted, hang containers from overhead beams; display succulents within frames as works of art; and attach pots, wreaths, or planted tubes to walls and fences. Such vertical gardens are beautiful when viewed from inside your home, provide privacy by creating a screen, make passageways and blank walls interesting, and surround you with greenery.

HANGING BASKETS

Succulents are better suited to hanging baskets than are the water-thirsty ornamentals typically planted in them and also require less maintenance. Vigilance is needed, however, to keep such containers looking their best—more pinching, pruning, and rotating than if the same plants were in terrestrial containers.

Traditional hanging baskets are made of wire and lined with dried moss, then filled with soil. Premade liners of coir (coconut fiber) are also available. During the hottest, driest part of the year, check such baskets often; they may need twice the water required by adjacent impermeable pots.

Watering wands—slender pipes that screw onto the end of a hose and are tipped with a bulb-shaped sprayer—make it possible to reach the tops of hanging baskets without standing on a ladder. The gentle spray ensures even distribution of water without disturbing the soil.

Or weave a drip irrigation tube down the chain that holds the basket, with an emitter on the end that drips according to a preprogrammed schedule.

For stability, a hanging pot or basket requires three heavy-gauge wires or chains attached to the rim, equidistant from each other and all the same length. Make sure the chain is strong enough that the rings will not separate due to the weight of the container. Secure the hook that holds the chains to a ceiling stud or overhead beam.

To balance sun exposure, rotate baskets 180 degrees every week or two. A fishing swivel between the ceiling hook and the loop above the chains makes it possible to turn the basket without having to detach and rehang it. The swivel consists of two metal rings with a barrel-shaped pivoting joint between them. (Its conventional use is to keep the line from twisting as a fish is reeled in.)

Succulents commonly used in hanging baskets include rosary vine (*Ceropegia woodii*), wax flower (hoya), *Sedum morganianum*, *Sedum burrito*, trailing senecios, and stacked crassulas. But any stem succulent is a possibility, because it will become pendant as it searches for soil in which to root.

Ice plants used as ground covers—such as *Aptenia cordifolia* (red apple ice plant), *Drosanthemum floribundum* (rosea ice plant), and *Ruschia deltoides*— also will work but may overwhelm other plants.

When you trim the plants, reinsert cuttings to enhance the arrangement's balance and fullness.

(left) This wire basket is lined with a nursery flat of sedum. The designer inverted the flat into the basket so that the plants face outward and the roots and soil are on the inside. She then filled the rest of the container with potting soil and added a rat-tail cactus, plus other cuttings that will cascade. Suzy Schaefer garden.

(right) A coir-lined basket holds string of pearls (*Senecio rowleyanus*). Art and Sandra Baldwin garden, San Diego, CA.

TUBE PLANTERS

Aquarium and water-feature designer Pat McWhinney of Garden Grove, California, needed a way to make prefab waterfalls look natural, so he came up with a socklike tube that can be snaked amid boulders and planted. The material is an industrial cloth that looks and feels like felt but is much stronger (its conventional use is as a vapor barrier for flooring). McWhinney, who has a seamstress sew the sleeves to whatever length he wants (with a diameter of 2, 4, or 6 inches), also improvised a machine that packs them with potting soil.

Applications for succulent-planted tubes include wreaths, garlands, freestanding columns (with a pole down the middle), and as strips tucked between the risers of outdoor stairs. Planted tubes also make beautiful vertical gardens—lush green tapestries that enhance small patios and create views from windows that look onto walls and fences.

To plant the tubes, McWhinney slits an opening in the fabric with a knife, makes a hole in the soil inside with a pointed metal dowel, inserts a cutting or small plant, then tucks moistened sphagnum moss around it to hold it in place. Given bright but not intense light and adequate moisture (via drip irrigation), cuttings soon root. As with a fountain, water might be collected, filtered, and recirculated.

(top) Planted tubes attached to a wall create a vertical garden. Design by Pat McWhinney.

(bottom) A planted tube garlands an echeveria-filled pot. R. C. and Beverly Cohen garden, Newport Beach, CA. Photo by Claire Curran.

(next page top) Rosette succulents grow in tubes lining gaps between risers. R. C. and Beverly Cohen garden.

(next page bottom) Collars of sphagnum moss prevent newly planted echeveria and crassula cuttings from falling out of a soil-filled cloth tube. Design by Pat McWhinney, Garden Grove, CA.

Plants in this eye-level grouping include graptoverias, a dasylirion, *Agave americana* 'Marginata', and *Crassula arborescens* (silver dollar jade). Chanticleer Garden, Wayne, PA. Photo by Rob Cardillo.

WALL POTS AND PLANTED WALLS

Wall pots enable the sculptural forms of succulents to be displayed against a solid background. One way to effectively fill a vertical space is to plant a sconce with an upright plant and another that trails.

Hang heavy pots from a screw that goes into a stud or use concrete nails to secure pots to the mortar between bricks. Before permanently attaching pots to a wall, make sure that it will not be stained or damaged by moisture or dripping water and that the pots can withstand freezing temperatures. If the plantings will be seasonal, choose pots that will look good on the wall even when empty.

(left) A talavera sconce planted with echeverias stands out against a white wall. Design by Jim Bishop, Bishop Garden Design.

(right) *Ruschia deltoides* forms a plume for a classical sconce. Claire and Jerry Parent residence, Santa Barbara, CA. Design by Sydney Baumgartner.

Soothing hues of peach and magenta combine to make a wall display. The frame holds chicken wire and sphagnum moss, in which *Crassula* 'Campfire' and other cuttings grow. Wehle-Lynch garden. Design by Marilee Kuhlmann, Comfort Zones Garden Design, Los Angeles, CA.

Stones a mere 1 inch thick form a facade that conceals concrete blocks underneath. Crassulas, echeverias, sedums, and aeoniums have rooted in moist sphagnum moss stuffed into cracks. Mujiba Cabugos garden, Santa Barbara, CA.

A stacked flagstone wall incorporates a flower-pot planted with *Sedum clavatum*. Above my dog is another embedded pot, with *Sedum* 'Blue Spruce'. Cambria Nursery and Florist, Cambria, CA. Design by Shana McCormick.

Cliff dwellers such as *Aeonium tabuliforme* and dudleyas, as well as sempervivums and any number of trailers, are suitable for tucking into the crevices of rock walls. As stems grow, threadlike roots emerge from leaf axils and anchor the plants.

Green walls, which consist of planted panels that generally are attached to the exterior of buildings, are an offspring of green roofs. Such installations need irrigation, ideally via hidden drip lines; are heavy and should be securely supported; require some method of drainage (if not allowed to drip into a flowerbed below); and, to protect the wall from moisture, should be backed with impermeable cloth.

Thousands of assorted sempervivum rosettes suggest an aerial photograph. The 80-by-60-inch vertical garden, which comprises a dozen 20-inch-square planted panels, was stored flat in a greenhouse for six months so the succulents would be well-rooted. The wood frame emphasizes that this is an artwork. Design by Robin Stockwell of Succulent Gardens and Kevin Smith of Flora Grubb Gardens nursery. Photo by Caitlin Atkinson.

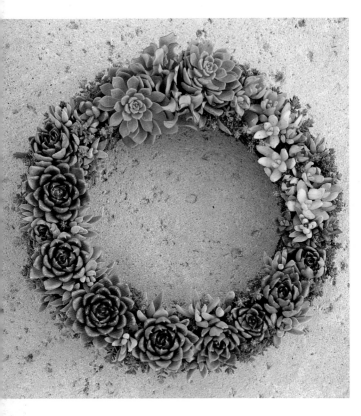

(left) Red sempervivums are aligned opposite cuttings of yellow *Sedum adolphi* and blue-green echeverias. Design by Linda Estrin Garden Design, Oak Park, CA.

(right) As plants grow, a succulent wreath will deconstruct. Aeoniums, crassulas, and graptopetalums appear to explode outward as they reach for the sun. Suzy Schaefer residence.

WREATHS

Succulent wreaths look good year-round and can serve as table centerpieces as well as fence, gate, and wall enhancements. They are living wreaths (the greenery they contain takes root and grows) and a type of topiary (a wire form stuffed with moss and planted).

At wreath-making parties in my garden, each guest fills a nursery flat with about 100 cuttings from jade plants, graptopetalums, *Kalanchoe pumila*, *Aeonium haworthii*, *Sedum rubrotinctum*, red apple ice plant, and *Senecio serpens*. We then assemble the wreaths on a table in the succulent sitting area. After taking their wreaths home, some friends keep them trimmed; others let the plants grow. One simply set her wreath atop potting soil in a wide, shallow pot, thereby creating an instant container garden.

Wreaths might be packed tightly with cuttings or have a lacy look. I like to decide whether a wreath will be comprised primarily of gray-green and blue-green foliage or brighter yellow-greens, and then select a few accent plants that contrast—such as rosy pink echeverias with gray-green *Aeonium*

haworthii. Wreaths need not be composed of a lot of different kinds of succulents or even have many colors; those made of one to three kinds of succulents, or that are monochromatic, are lovely.

Wreath frames of heavy gauge wire, available at hobby and crafts stores,
open like clamshells into two cylindrical troughs. Line each with moist
sphagnum moss and mound one side with potting soil, or plant cuttings into
tightly packed moss. (Professional designers use green sphagnum moss
sold by the bale by florists' suppliers.) Wrap the doughnut-shaped form
with copper wire to hold it shut. Add two sturdy loops to the back—at top
and bottom—from which to hang the wreath, so it can be rotated for even
sun exposure.

Colorful cuttings in a florist-
designed wreath include
variegated aeoniums, lav-
ender graptopetalums, and
red-tipped jade. Resembling
striped ribbons at lower right
are *Cryptanthus acaulis* bromeliads. Chicweed. Design by Susan and
Melissa Teisl and Leah Winetz.

(left) With the addition of a candle, a wreath (atop a pot saucer) serves as a table centerpiece. *Mon Petit Chou, Encinitas, CA. Design by Bonnie Manion.*

(right) A wreath packed solidly with sphagnum moss holds cuttings planted in distinct and colorful sections. Pink, white, and green *Sedum* 'Tricolor' is at 5 and 7 o'clock. Thick sempervivum stems were pared to carrotlike points before insertion. *The Original Living Wreath. Design by Margee Rader.*

Plant the form with cuttings that average 2 or 3 inches long (remove lowest leaves). Use a chopstick or pencil to poke holes into the moss, and long-handled tweezers to grasp and insert the stems. If you do not want to wait for cuttings to root before hanging the wreath, secure them with florists' pins. Otherwise, lay the wreath flat in filtered sunlight for several weeks and keep moist but not soggy. Should the moss dry out, rehydrate it by filling a clean trash can lid with water and setting the wreath in it to soak.

TOPIARIES

A succulent wreath is a topiary, but a topiary need not be a wreath. Wire topiary forms ready to be stuffed with moss (some even come prestuffed) are available via mail order. To locate them online, type "topiary frame" into an Internet search engine. Shapes include dogs, cats, butterflies, spheres, and cones.

The Versailles architecture of the Rosecliff mansion museum, a venue for the Newport Flower Show, inspired members of Rhode Island's Plum Beach Garden Club to create an 8-foot topiary cone planted with rosette succulents. Four 1-½-inch-square pine balusters, mitered to a central

An *Aeonium haworthii* rosette suggests a bow at the clasp of a purse; jade cuttings outline the sides. A grid of copper wire holds moss in place. The Original Living Wreath. Design by Margee Rader.

Senecio radicans 'Fish Hooks' wraps the handle of the completed topiary purse.

Echeveria rosettes suggest a china teapot's floral pattern. Grewsome Gardens nursery, Bellingham, WA. Design by Cleo Pirtle. Photo by Terri Collins.

The ears, legs, and tail of a topiary terrier are watch-chain crassula. The Original Living Wreath. Design by Margee Rader.

4-inch-diameter pipe, form the support structure. It sits atop a white box of synthetic wood that is impervious to water. The balusters were wrapped with burlap and chicken wire, then stapled into place, leaving a gap at the top so the cone could be filled with potting soil. Into slits cut in the burlap, club members inserted 600 succulent cuttings—mostly sempervivums, but also echeverias and sedums. The club's topiary obelisk won a blue ribbon at the Newport Flower Show.

This topiary cone planted with rosette succulents was created by members of Rhode Island's Plum Beach Garden Club. Design by Sue Shriner, Priscilla Green, and Anne O'Neill. Photo by Robin Lee Reed.

Containers tightly packed with cuttings have a lush look similar to florists' arrangements. EuroAmerican Propagators. Design by Margee Rader.

FLORAL-STYLE ARRANGEMENTS

Like floral arrangements, tightly packed pots of succulent cuttings make beautiful gifts, centerpieces, and party favors. And when aligned in rows or in concentric circles, small plants or cuttings create intriguing geometric compositions. One designer compares working with succulents to sculpting, because the leaves of many resemble clay.

In a conventional floral arrangement, the height of plant material is one and a half times the diameter of the container. A succulent arrangement is of necessity more compact; although they look like flowers, fleshy rosettes are not airy blooms atop slender stems.

Leaves of succulents may appear rubbery, but they are not flexible. Do not insert the stems into the sharp, pointed tips of a floral frog, which will crush tissues, inhibit root formation, and invite rot. Live plant material will soon deconstruct an arrangement unless new growth is pinched back. It is best to consider floral-style succulent arrangements temporary—even though they may last months (if not overwatered), and cuttings eventually may root in an arrangement's moss, soil, or floral foam.

A pink-blooming *Kalanchoe blossfeldiana* inspired an arrangement that includes pink-edged aeoniums and echeverias. White-webbed *Sempervivum arachnoideum* rosettes add contrast. California Cactus Center nursery. Design by Arree Thongthiraj.

In a holiday centerpiece, cream-and-green *Aeonium* 'Suncup' rosettes surround a red-tipped echeveria. Chicweed.

(top) A stacked crassula on the left balances the cascading sedum on the right. Terra Sol Garden Center, Santa Barbara, CA. Design by Tony Krock.

(above) *Sedum burrito* makes a good fringe for echeverias (left), as do sempervivums for aeoniums (lower right). Succulent Gardens nursery, Castroville, CA. Design by Robin Stockwell.

(left) A wrought-iron wall embellishment serves as a backdrop for a pot of green and 'Sunburst' aeoniums, and blue echeverias. Roger's Gardens nursery, Corona del Mar, CA.

(below) *Aeonium arboreum* 'Zwartkop' rosettes in the center of a trough repeat its dark color, and *Sedum burrito* and *Senecio rowleyanus* trail over its edge. Chicweed.

Both arrangements are newly planted. On the left, a columnar *Pachycereus marginatus* (Mexican fence post) lends height; contrasting with it are succulents that repeat its color yet have different forms and texture. In the pot on the right, *Euphorbia tirucalli* (pencil plant) and *Crassula ovata* 'Hummel's Sunset' serve as a backdrop for rosette succulents. Solana Succulents nursery, Solana Beach, CA. Design by Jeff Moore.

Floral-style arrangements might be symmetrical or asymmetrical, but all elements should balance. This means objects on either side of the center are roughly equal in weight—a term that refers more to their visual impact than avoirdupois. A tall aeonium on one side might balance a cascading burro tail sedum on the other. Dark colors are heavier than light.

Decide which side of the arrangement will face the viewer, or if it will be seen from all sides. Position the focal point at or near the center of the composition (or, if off center, provide a balancing element), then arrange the remaining plant material as though erupting naturally and exuberantly from a garden, radiating upward and outward. Allow at least one leaf or stem to extend over the pot's edge to break its hard line, but do not let cascading foliage completely conceal the rim.

Dish gardens by Jeff Moore, owner of Solana Succulents nursery in Solana Beach, California, blend elements of floral arrangements and miniature landscapes. Moore's eclectic combos—each of which he assembles in about 15 minutes—are meant to be viewed from a main vantage point. Larger succulents suggesting trees and shrubs go in back; smaller ones, which repeat or contrast elements of the larger, in front. Rocks enhance the composition and hold plants in place, and gravel serves as a topdressing.

THOMAS HOBBS'S SUCCULENT CONTAINERS

Thomas Hobbs of Vancouver, British Columbia, a former florist who co-owns Southlands Nursery, pioneered the use of succulents in floral-style arrangements and popularized the concept of the "succulent pizza"—large pot saucers planted with echeverias. Hobbs overwinters his succulents indoors beginning around November 1, then brings them out in spring, at which time he creates in-ground and dish gardens afresh.

When designing "a jewel box of horticultural treasures," Hobbs favors succulents with intriguing textures and metallic or iridescent hues. In addition to echeverias, he uses kalanchoes, sedums, aloes, orostachys, jovibarbas, and sempervivums, which he packs tightly. Rosettes often are of various sizes and shapes, with one or two large ones serving as the composition's focal point.

Hobbs hints at the way succulents resemble undersea flora by incorporating shells, brain coral, and the skeletal tracery of fan coral; fist-sized lumps of glass; and glazed ceramic balls that resemble sea urchins. He also mixes strings of beads with succulents that cascade from urns, thereby suggesting exotic vines.

Seasonal pots of succulents at the home of Thomas Hobbs in Vancouver, BC, are densely planted and precisely arranged. Seashells and coral lend whimsy. Photo by Rob Cardillo.

Posts of half-inch-diameter, hollow copper tubing extend upward from the corners of tall pots. Rubber pads cushion glass disks that serve as small patio tables. The green pot holds a caruncled (knobby) echeveria. Barrels & Branches nursery, Encinitas, CA.

(left) Twelve round opuntia paddles are aligned in a shallow, rectangular pot. A red topdressing repeats the plants' red topknots. California Cactus Center nursery. Design by Arree Thongthiraj.

(right) *Echeveria imbricata* rosettes crowd each other and echo the shape of their pot. Design by Molly Wood Garden Design, Costa Mesa, CA.

Few compositions are as captivating as those that emphasize the inherent symmetry of succulents. Pots that are square or round lend themselves to geometric arrangements of astrophytums, rebutia, mammillaria, globular euphorbias, cereus, opuntia, *Crassula perforata*, and succulents with tight rosettes (such as aeoniums, echeverias, and sempervivums).

Growing succulents in glass containers makes it possible to place arrangements on wood tabletops and other surfaces that might be damaged by the

(left) *Haworthia attenuata* grows in recycled plastic bottles. The Juicy Leaf, Venice, CA. Design by Felix Navarro.

(right) A windowsill-sized glass container holds echeverias. Design by Felix Navarro.

moisture that normally collects beneath pots. Glass presents several challenges: to not overwater the plants because there is no drainage; to not allow moisture to collect inside the container where sunlight will hit it, potentially fostering algae growth; and to make sure sun magnified by the glass does not burn the plants.

Felix Navarro, owner of The Juicy Leaf in Venice, California, creates gardens of succulents in glass vases, bowls, and cylinders. The plants grow in inner pots made from cut-in-half, recycled plastic bottles filled with potting soil. Glossy pebbles, crushed rock, or sand—sometimes stratified for design interest—conceal the plastic pots. Navarro recommends applying a minimal amount of water (about one ounce) to the base of each plant every 15 to 20 days, taking care not to moisten the pebble layer.

HOLIDAYS AND SPECIAL OCCASIONS

On Valentine's Day, give your sweetie rosette-shaped succulents in a red-glazed pot or heart-shaped container. Come spring, fill an Easter basket with egg-shaped *Euphorbia obesa*. For a conversation-starting Thanksgiving centerpiece, plant a cornucopia with colorful ruffled echeverias. In December, decorate an agave or aloe with red glass balls, then take a photo of it for your holiday greeting cards.

When they reflect an event's theme and color palette, succulent cuttings in small matching pots make appealing party favors. For a wedding reception, instead of a large centerpiece at each table, group several smaller ones, so each guest or couple can take one home.

Whenever you find good-looking coffee mugs at discount stores, buy a few to keep on hand to use to make small succulent arrangements for party favors and hostess gifts. Let the design and color of the mug inspire the shape, texture, and color of the cuttings you choose. Fill the mug with floral foam (Oasis) that has been soaked and trimmed to fit the container snugly. Remove lower leaves from cuttings so stems will insert easily into the foam. If stems are fragile, make holes with a toothpick, pencil, or chopstick. Use enough cuttings to conceal the foam and to create a pleasing bouquet.

(left) A Valentine pot of succulents that resemble flowers includes aeoniums, sempervivums, *Echeveria* 'Perle von Nurnberg' and 'Doris Taylor', and *Echeveria affinis* 'Black Prince'. California Cactus Center nursery. Design by Sue Thongthiraj.

(right) Sedum cuttings grow in tightly packed moss. EuroAmerican Propagators. Design by Margee Rader.

A gumlike adhesive secures an angel ornament to a leaf of *Agave americana* 'Mediopicta Alba' (tuxedo agave).

Red glass balls call attention to the orange margins of *Aloe striata* (coral aloe) leaves.

Small pots decorated with blue china birds await a spring garden event. Chicweed.

A topiary tree—anchored by vertical wires that extend into the pot—consists of a wire cone stuffed with sphagnum moss and planted with graduated sizes of sempervivums. The Original Living Wreath. Design by Margee Rader.

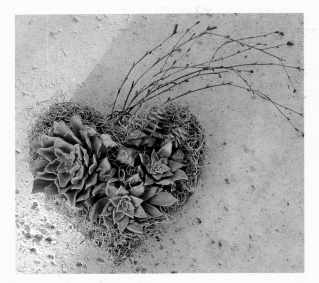

A composition consisting primarily of echeverias includes *Crassula perforata* cuttings and slender dried twigs. Spanish moss adds texture and fills gaps. Design and photo by Linda Estrin.

LINDA ESTRIN'S HEARTS

Garden designer Linda Estrin of Oak Park, California, fashions heart-shaped containers using ½-inch wire mesh available at hardware stores. She lines the bottom and sides with salvaged window screen and may add a layer of florists' fabric (one brand is Art-Mesh), sold by the roll online and in crafts stores.

Estrin chooses the plants first and experiments with combinations of colors, forms, and textures, all the while keeping scale and proportion in mind—similar to how she might design an actual garden. The mesh holds in the soil well enough that it does not dry out rapidly, so her compositions need only a light sprinkling once a week or so (depending on the time of year and the weather). She applies no fertilizer because she does not want the plants to grow rapidly.

A heart is one of many shapes that might be fashioned from wire mesh. Design by Linda Estrin.

An aeonium rosette grows in a teacup. The Water Conservation Garden at Cuyamaca College, El Cajon, CA.

A cracked coffee mug holds sedeveria, sedum, and crassula cuttings. Garden Glories Nursery, Vista, CA. Design by Liz Youngflesh.

The low-light arrangement on the left contains mostly haworthias; the one on the right, several types of sansevierias and haworthias, plus string of pearls. In the pot in back are a variegated hoya and red *Cryptanthus acaulis* bromeliads. Chicweed.

You might put a mug arrangement at each place setting; arrange them equidistant along a buffet; or tie helium balloons to their handles and use them to decorate the guest of honor's gift table.

If you chip or crack a treasured teacup or mug, do not discard it. Fill it with potting soil and plant it with one or more rosette-shaped succulents. If the cup has a saucer, attach it securely (use china glue or a glue gun) so the two form a unit. Place on an outdoor table, as though awaiting a tête-à-tête.

Bowls of low-light succulents make good gifts for office workers and others who spend much of their time indoors. Such arrangements might include haworthias, sansevierias, hoyas, string of pearls (*Senecio rowleyanus*), kitten paws (*Cotyledon tomentosa*), *Crassula multicava*, and bright gold *Sedum makinoi* 'Ogon'.

MINIATURE LANDSCAPES

Any container planted with succulents is a miniature garden, but a miniature landscape is different; it engages the imagination by presenting a tiny world that invites exploration. A well-done miniature landscape is credible yet magical.

A diminutive landscape that incorporates rocks and trees (or treelike plants) is a form of *penjing* (literally "tray scenery"), an ancient Chinese art form that preceded the Japanese art of bonsai. Depending on the type and shape of the rocks, they might represent mountains, boulders, cliffs, or even a reef.

When designing a miniature landscape, think of the composition as a perspective drawing in three dimensions. Place larger rocks and plants in the back and those that are smaller in front, to create a sense of distance. If you will be stacking rocks, you might enhance their stability by securing them with masonry adhesive (sold at home improvement stores).

The secret of designing a convincing miniature landscape is to envision what it might be like if you were small enough, yourself, to experience it. For example, if you are attempting to create mountainous terrain, imagine a hiker in the setting, his boots crunching a gravelly path underfoot, one hand shading his eyes as he picks his way between boulders. When a rock formation halts his progress, he looks for a way around it. He gazes upward and spots elevations that he would like to explore. When he cannot see around a corner, the unknown entices him. As he approaches a pinnacle, he may or may not decide to climb it. He looks for flat rocks that provide resting places where he can sit and enjoy the view.

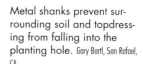
Metal shanks prevent surrounding soil and topdressing from falling into the planting hole. Gary Bartl, San Rafael, CA.

Choose succulents for miniature landscapes that do not grow rapidly, lest the scale of the composition quickly become compromised. A 4-inch *Agave americana* pup may start out in correct proportion to a miniature building, but soon the structure will look odd alongside an overly large succulent. (*Haworthia attenuata*, which has an agave-like shape, is a better choice.) Keep in mind that the bigger the container, the more room plants have to spread their roots, which promotes growth.

Because plants are constantly changing and do not always grow in the direction you want them to, a miniature landscape will need more pruning and tending than a succulent-filled container that does not attempt to suggest a fantasy world. To add a plant without disturbing other elements of the composition, one designer hammers thin metal shanks (4 to 6 inches long and similar to hacksaw blades) into the ground to skirt the planting area, leaving one side open for access. He scoops dirt out of the hole with a spackling knife, then lowers the new plant into place with long-handled tweezers. After he fills the hole with soil and tamps it, he removes the shanks, then adds topdressing as needed to repair the surface.

Miniature worlds might also incorporate small houses, toy vehicles, animals, and people. Look for these in secondhand shops, import stores, crafts stores, and holiday boutiques; and from suppliers of accessories for dollhouses, garden railways, and aquariums. Seal any item made of a permeable material with clear polyurethane. Fine sand looks good as a topdressing, but crushed rock is often better because it does not scatter as readily when splashed. To efficiently water plants in a miniature landscape, use a watering can with a long, narrow spout.

It is intriguing to see how various designers create miniature worlds using succulents, each with very different styles. The examples here take you to Guatemala, a mountainous wilderness, the desert, and beneath the ocean's surface.

Guatemalan scene

At a store that imports Guatemalan folk art, artist and succulent collector Suzy Schaefer finds miniature terracotta buildings that evoke the American Southwest and Latin America. In wide, shallow terracotta pots, Schaefer positions the tiny buildings in front of jade cuttings that resemble large trees, atop a piece of slate, which protects the structures from moisture in the soil and keeps them level. She then adds one or more large rocks to suggest rugged terrain. Additional cuttings of graptopetalums and aeoniums go in the background; and in the foreground, small-leaved succulents such as *Sedum rubrotinctum* and *Othonna capensis*.

When preparing to create a composition in a large (3-foot-wide) pot, Schaefer cuts a circle the same diameter as the pot from newspaper and takes the template with her to a nursery, where she spreads it on the ground. She arranges potted succulents atop it to determine how many she needs and to see how they look together. She does not pack the container, preferring to fine-tune the design as plants grow and fill in.

To vary the terrain in my own Schaefer-inspired landscape, I created a hillock in the foreground with rocks and gravel from the garden. Cuttings include *Aloe nobilis*, *Faucaria tigrina*, *Sedum rubrotinctum*, and *Echeveria pulvinata*.

(next page) *Crassula ovata* behind the tiny building is in bloom, sedums and othonna fill the foreground, and a rock with interesting striations suggests a mountain. Design by Suzy Schaefer.

A toy MINI Cooper inspired the choice of the pot, which also is yellow, as are bits of glass in the topdressing. Pot-ted, Los Angeles, CA. Design by Anna Goeser.

Chips of turquoise glass, a car the same color, and a doll-sized red-and-white umbrella accessorize a swimming-pool-in-the-desert diorama. To the left of the car is *Opuntia* 'Desert Gem'; in the back, suggesting a Joshua tree, a diminutive cholla; and in the foreground, a cluster of rebutia. Pot-ted. Design by Anna Goeser.

Desert dioramas

Anna Goeser of Los Angeles is a self-described junk collector fond of mid-century collectibles. Goeser, who makes one-of-a-kind arrangements to order (clients are "the acting community; they like kitschy stuff"), first composed dish gardens to provide a garden shop's customers with pot-and-plant ideas. Her cactus compositions reminded her of trips to the desert but they looked a little desolate, so she started adding diminutive roads, cars, and people. "Before I knew it, I was making little worlds," she says. Goeser calls her designs Mojave bonsai.

Her inspiration might originate with accessories or a pot's bright color, but all items look retro. Newly minted thumb-sized cars, although readily available, do not as effectively encapsulate the mid-20th-century fantasies Goeser attempts to create. Bauer pottery in bright colors also enhances the back-in-time feel.

Succulent seascapes

Sea-themed succulentscapes capitalize on the resemblance that many of the plants bear to ocean flora. To immerse viewers in your underwater scene, place one or more lava rocks or chunks of coral so they extend steeply upward. Surround them with cylindrical euphorbias, rat-tail cactus, dyckias, small agaves and aloes, stacked crassulas, and crested or monstrose succulents—to name a few of many possibilities.

Props are important: rusted gears, a fan of coral, or one or more brightly colored wood or plastic fish atop stiff wire stems add verisimilitude to the scene. For a topdressing, use crushed lava rock, pebbles, marbles, or tumbled glass.

(left) A blue-painted wooden fish atop a thin metal rod appears to swim through *Euphorbia tirucalli* 'Sticks on Fire'. *Crassula perfoliata* 'Morgan's Beauty' is at bottom; *Euphorbia flanaganii* at left; and a crested euphorbia at right, alongside a lava rock. Solana Succulents nursery. Design by Jeff Moore.

(right) A crested cactus, egg-shaped and crested euphorbias, cascading baby's necklace, and lava rocks suggest an undersea reef. Solana Succulents nursery. Design by Jeff Moore.

The boat is a prototype for one the designer's husband plans to build; they enjoy the humor of it being full of holes. Plants include semper-vivums, sedums, and woolly thyme. Pebbles and drift-wood came from a nearby beach. Design and photo by Mari Malcolm, Seattle, WA. Boat sculpture by Andrew Malcolm.

A thumb-sized china turtle swims through glass beads in various hues of blue, in a seascape of red-tipped *Crassula schmidtii* and *Echeveria agavoides* rosettes. Terra Sol Garden Center. Design by Tony Krock.

(left) When viewed from the front, thin sheets of flagstone resemble overlapping mountains. Design by Gary Bartl, San Rafael, CA.

(right) As he grooms one of his Sierrascapes, Gary Bartl uses long-handled tweezers to reposition a small rock. Plants include euphorbias, senecios, haworthias, gasterias, and living stones.

Sierrascapes

Sierrascapes by Gary Bartl of San Rafael, California, suggest California's Sierra Nevada range and have many more rocks than plants. Fist-sized stones look like immense boulders, and crushed lava rock paves what appear to be rugged hiking trails. Amid rocks, on several levels, are pockets of plants.

To create a Sierrascape, Bartl fills a large container with a gritty mixture of commercial potting soil and lava sand. (He uses a higher percentage of lava sand for plants such as lithops that require exceptional drainage and drier soil.) Bartl packs the pot tightly with potting mix so it will not compress later on and cause the composition to sink or shift. He also mounds the soil to create hills and valleys.

Bartl positions the largest, most imposing rocks first, burying them so they are well anchored. Thin sheets of rock chiseled from slabs of flagstone jut upward like mountains; these have colorations ranging from rose through shades of rust and pale yellow. Additional rocks create arroyos, crevices, and cliffs.

Once rocks are in place, he adds plants: *Euphorbia leucodendron* cuttings (which have upright, cylindrical branches); dwarf forms of *Euphorbia milii*; small, spherical *Euphorbia obesa* (effective when clustered); blue *Senecio serpens*; pine-tree-like *Crassula tetragona*; and *Adromischus*, among other succulents.

STAGING

Collectors of cacti and succulents combine a passion for the plants—especially rare and unusual ones—with a desire to cultivate and display perfect specimens. *Staging* is a term collectors use to describe the art of presenting a container-grown plant so its attributes are evident and amplified. This involves selecting the proper pot, correctly positioning the plant within it, and adding topdressing and/or rocks to create a living work of art. Thanks to the Cactus and Succulent Society of America (CSSA) and its affiliates, which host juried shows throughout the United States and beyond, collectors are rewarded for their efforts, and the public can see their skillfully staged compositions.

Although many staged plants at cactus and succulent shows have been bonsai'd—dwarfed through repeated pruning of limbs and roots—the primary goal of staging is not to create a miniature landscape nor to stunt the plant but rather to suggest (and idealize) how it might look in its natural habitat.

At juried shows, staged entries are evaluated by experts and receive ribbons or trophies based on merit. The Inter-City Cactus and Succulent Show, held annually at the Los Angeles Arboretum in Arcadia, California, is the largest and most prestigious in the world. Entries compete for a maximum of 100 points: 60 for the condition of the plant, 20 for its staging, 15 for the plant's size and maturity, and 5 for accuracy of nomenclature.

When explaining judging criteria, certified CSSA judges Michael Buckner of San Diego and Woody Minnich of New Mexico noted that a well-staged entry's plant, pot, and topdressing are greater than the sum of its parts. A staged pot must be uncontrived; gnomes, tiny bridges, and similarly unnatural elements are anathema—and will relegate an entry to the category of

Blue-ribbon *Haworthia retusa ×splendens.* Inter-City Cactus and Succulent Show. Design by Arnold Chaney.

dish gardens (which also tend to have more than one type of plant). Additionally, judges consider the difficulty of cultivation, encourage novices, and deduct points if a plant is untidy (sporting dead leaves, a weed, pests, or a spiderweb) or if a botanical name (such as *Ariocarpus kotschoubeyanus*) is misspelled.

Staging has evolved considerably in the United States over the past 30 years. It used to be that only the plants mattered; it was not uncommon for a rare and valuable astrophytum, echeveria, or haworthia to be shown in a plastic pot or rusty can. Now containers are integral to the overall presentation, and the investment collectors make in pots is significant. Even so, a truly exceptional plant in a poor container may still earn an award, and it is considered bad form for a snazzy pot to draw attention away from the plant.

A well-staged cluster of *Deuterocohnia brevifolia* (syn. *Abromeitiella brevifolia*) at the Inter-City Show. Design by Larry Grammer.

Agave parryi 'Cream Spike' appears to grow from a rocky outcropping. California Cactus Center nursery. Design by Larry Grammer.

The majority of containers are in subdued earth tones—shades of brown, rust, beige, and tan—with a matte finish rather than glossy. Handcrafted pots predominate. Among them are containers made of clay that, when soft, were impressed by the artist with random lines or geometric patterns, then hand molded into vessels shaped like a gathered purse but wider at the top. Echoing the color of the plant with that of its pot is called monochromatic staging, but there seldom are any pink, red, purple, orange, bright yellow, or chartreuse pots among trophy winners. Blue is an exception; according to Minnich, dark blue and cobalt glazes lend elegance to pots, contrast with foliage and make it brighter, and subconsciously connote a first-place ribbon.

An estimated 95 percent of award-winning entries have been in the same pot for years, and many of those venerable specimens were exhibited at previous shows. Plants change over time, so pruning and staging are ongoing. When a cactus or succulent outgrows its pot, the owner may repot the plant in a larger container or prune the roots and return the plant to the same container (thereby creating a bonsai). Some plants, such as ficus, grow rapidly; others may not need repotting for years. Fresh soil revitalizes the plant and promotes growth that the owner will trim and train to create an even better entry for subsequent shows.

Enthusiast Larry Grammer has won numerous awards at cactus and succulent shows for his staged pots, which he also makes for California Cactus Center nursery in Pasadena, California. Influences on Grammer's design aesthetic include a college major in commercial art; traveling in Mexico and seeing how cacti and succulents grow in rugged terrain; and observing potters at the Laguna Beach, California, art colony.

Grammer selects a container in proportion to the plant that suits its shape, chooses a topdressing that appears natural and has merit in terms of texture and color, and juxtaposes the plant with rocks that may also serve to anchor it. He tends to place plants off center and to rotate rosettes forward so that they are elevated at a slight angle to face the viewer (who thereby is spared having to stand directly over them to admire their beauty and symmetry). This tilted aspect is also typical of plants in habitat. Yet tipping a newly potted succulent creates a dilemma: the plant's root-ball is exposed in the back, and its leaves dip below the soil in front. Grammer's solution is to elevate the entire plant slightly, tucking rocks between leaves and roots in back, and between leaves and soil in front. In addition to holding the plant in place, the rocks—which themselves are ornamental—become part of the composition.

(above) *Portulacaria afra*, trained and scored, at a nursery.
Design by Tom Jesch, Daylily Hill nursery, Escondido, CA.

(right) *Portulacaria afra* 'Variegata' grows amid rocks that resemble rugged terrain. The plant is naturally pendant, so these cuttings had to be trained upright. Design by Rudy Lime, San Diego, CA.

BONSAI

A wonderful hobby for collectors with limited space, bonsai is as absorbing as in-ground gardening, requires no land or physical exertion, and offers the creative rewards (and challenges) inherent in sculpting and perfecting a living plant. Bonsai'd succulents generally are grown hard, meaning they are toughened through sun exposure that stops just short of burning and they receive no fertilizer and only enough water to survive. Such harsh conditions make plants more rugged and their leaves smaller. (Nursery plants, on the other hand, are grown soft—in bright but not intense light, with ample water and fertilizer—to encourage lush and rapid growth.)

Rudy Lime, a longtime member of the San Diego Cactus and Succulent Society, has spent decades perfecting the use of succulents as bonsai. When choosing a subject, he looks for plants (or limbs, if taking cuttings) that are thick at the base and taper upward. He also recommends starting with overgrown garden succulents. Woody ice plants, for example, can be trimmed to reveal a gnarled trunk, then root-pruned, potted, and trained into majestic little trees with shimmering blooms.

Jade plants, *Sedum oxypetalum*, and *Portulacaria afra* are good for beginners; all respond well to cutting and training, are shrub forming, have naturally treelike branching structures, are inexpensive and readily available, and start effortlessly from cuttings. The plants produce rewarding results in a relatively short time but do not rapidly overgrow their pots. Consider more interesting kinds of *Crassula ovata* than the common green one—perhaps golden-leaved 'Hummel's Sunset'; spoon-leaved 'Hobbit'; or 'Crosby's Compact', which resembles the species but is smaller overall. Aptly named bonsai crassula (*Crassula sarcocaulis*) has textural bark, tiny leaves, and the added benefit of being frost hardy.

Portulacaria limbs, unlike those of crassulas, do not snap off easily and can be broken so that they angle downward yet still are attached. As a limb heals, exposed tissue at the elbow will be corded and knotty. Also, the trunk can be scored to create scarred ridges that suggest weathering.

A phrase bonsai enthusiasts use is "the plant has to earn its pot." Because pairing your succulent bonsai with the right pot is an important decision, grow new plants (or rooted cuttings) in nursery pots for a year or more, all the while trimming and training the plants. Then pick a pot that complements their emerging forms. This might be round or oval, square or rectangular, shallow or columnar, glazed or terracotta. Simple is best; the container's job is to provide a suitable, subtle frame.

Soft wire sold by the roll from suppliers of bonsai tools can be coiled into a sleeve that gently molds limbs and guides growth. If limbs are too close together, separate them by wrapping the lower one with wire and hanging fishing weights on it to pull it downward. Or use pieces of soft wood notched so they can be wedged between branches to push them apart.

When pruning, keep the tree you are creating in mind. Aim for a loosely structured cone, which is the shape trees grow into as they expose as much foliage as possible to sunlight. Structure is more important than leaves; a near-leafless bonsai is successful if it creates the illusion of a much larger tree. Austerity and elegance are preferable to lushness.

Use slender clippers with a curved tip that allow you to maneuver into the branches and make precision cuts. If you are uncertain whether to trim new

Woody ice plants make beautiful bonsai, as illustrated by *Drosanthemum crassum.* Design by Rudy Lime.

Woody ice plants make beautiful bonsai, as illustrated by *Drosanthemum crassum.* Design by Rudy Lime.

growth at the ends of limbs, decide if it enhances the overall shape of the plant or will eventually detract from it. New growth will branch from limbs that are cut, causing denser, thicker leaves. To channel this in the desired direction, make a slanted cut that slices through the growth node on the unwanted side.

If the plant is not well anchored after its roots have been pruned, use pliable wire or cable ties to temporarily secure it to its pot. Rocks that resemble boulders are also useful to prop up plants and prevent roots from lifting. Cover bare soil with a simple topdressing or plant a fine-leaved sedum to suggest moss. Do not use moss itself, as it needs moist growing conditions and the combination with succulents would not occur naturally.

Some of the most remarkable plants at cactus and succulent shows are bonsai with exposed and elevated roots. This lends character and interest to the composition, and presents the plant for better viewing, as a pedestal might. Plants that sit high atop exposed roots usually have been elevated incrementally, perhaps three or four times. Like classical bonsai, such presentations suggest trees weathered by wind and water.

Adenium swazicum, trained for 30 years, won both a blue ribbon and a judges' choice award at the Inter-City Show. Design by Peter Walkowiak. Pot by Mark Muradian.

Euphorbia ×grandicornis, now large, was started from seed in 1988. The actual stem (where roots and arms join) is a mere 3 inches in diameter. Every year the plant produces new branches from the top center. Inter-City Cactus and Succulent Show. Design by Peter Walkowiak.

Exposed roots of a 20-year-old *Ficus palmeri* appear to have captured a boulder. The Plant Man nursery, San Diego, CA. Design by Michael Buckner.

HOW TO ELEVATE ROOTS

Because what is hidden by soil is unknown, enthusiasts say that revealing a bonsai prospect's roots is like unwrapping a gift. CSSA judge and nurseryman Michael Buckner recommends *Ficus palmeri* for beginners. Here are his suggestions for plant selection and staging:

❋ Choose a 5-gallon nursery plant that is pot-bound but healthy, with plenty of lower foliage, and that has the look of a much larger tree. Ideally, it has a nice crown, with good aerial roots and leaves that are not large.

❋ Prune away two-thirds of the top growth and thin the rest.

❋ Slide the tree out of its pot and, directing the water pressure with your thumb, use a hose to blow out the soil below the trunk.

❋ Prune the roots and thread the upper ones through and around rocks that resemble boulders, leaving a bottom layer of 3 or 4 inches of roots and soil intact.

❋ Position the plant, with its roots somewhat raised and its most desirable side facing the viewer, in a bonsai-type pot.

❋ Add potting soil, then top-dress with decomposed granite or a similar crushed rock that suits the composition.

❋ Place the plant in filtered light. Raised roots are especially susceptible to sunburn and dehydration when first revealed.

Part Four

PLANTING, CARE, AND PROPAGATION

Offsets of this agave have expanded to the point where they have broken the container. Their leaves are already photosynthesizing.

"Y ou do not learn from your successes," observed a cactus and succulent show judge, discussing plant care and cultivation.

Indeed, nothing shocks a gardener into an awareness of what not to do quicker than a damaged or dying plant. Fortunately, succulents tend to be forgiving, but occasionally a simple mistake proves fatal. For example, after I left a treasured *Euphorbia obesa* (a beautiful little ball with herringbone stripes) out in the rain, I discovered how quickly plump succulents rot when waterlogged. At first, the obesa appeared fine, but within a week, it had collapsed like a deflated balloon. This taught me, in a way words could not, the perils of soggy soil.

At my presentations on designing with succulents, I am often asked for advice on soil, sun, water, fertilizer, and pests. Invariably, I begin with "it depends." Although the basic rules are simple (plant in well-drained soil, give bright light, protect from frost, keep warm and on the dry side, fertilize minimally, provide good air circulation), it is impossible to generalize about a category of plants that includes hundreds of genera and thousands of species. Furthermore, advice appropriate for gardeners who live in Texas may not be helpful to those in Oregon.

In any case, precise formulas are unnecessary. It has been my experience—having spent two decades growing, and occasionally neglecting, everything from annuals to orchids—that succulents are the simplest. Granted, I garden in Southern California, with low humidity, average annual rainfall of 15 inches, and decomposed granite soil. But my area (in the foothills, inland) has a temperature range from below freezing to over 100 degrees F. Many succulents cannot tolerate such extremes, yet the extra care they require has been minimal compared to other ornamental nonnatives.

Cacti and succulents have remarkable survival skills. If you have taken cuttings from succulents and then been too busy to plant them, doubtless you have observed that weeks and even months later, they look the same except perhaps for aerial roots that have formed along the stems. It seems the thicker the cuticle (skin) and the fleshier the leaves, the longer a cutting will survive. In my own garden, cuttings of *Senecio mandraliscae* sat in a basket in the shade for six weeks, waiting to be planted; the entire time, their appearance did not change.

During occasional periods of neglect (no water for several months) in the past, the leaves of a jade plant I have owned for decades shriveled. When given water, the plant revived and its leaves plumped. Several years ago, I moved it to where it would be watered by a sprinkler programmed to come on weekly. The plant subsequently grew too large for its pot, and the weight of its branches caused it to overturn. I left it where it lay, and new growth is at right angles to the rest of the plant. Some day it may make a wonderful, windblown-looking bonsai—if it has not rooted into the garden.

I mention such lapses to reassure you that you, too, can relax where succulents are concerned. Forget to water them, and they will adjust. Give them too much, and they will be fine unless waterlogged. Some people simply water them once a week in summer and once a month in winter, and do not bother with fertilizer at all.

Consider this chapter's suggestions for care and cultivation in light of your own region, growing conditions, and plants. Then apply common sense based on observation.

SUN EXPOSURE

Protect your potted succulents from hot, scorching sun. Even desert dwellers such as agaves and cacti, especially when small, are sheltered in their native habitats by rocky outcroppings or grow alongside larger shrubs that screen the sun for much of the day.

As a general rule, succulents do not need more than three or four hours of direct sun daily. But when determining the amount of light the plants should receive or can tolerate, bear in mind the time of year and whether they are dormant or actively growing. New growth appears at the tips of stems or the centers of rosettes and is brighter in color or coppery compared to the rest of the plant. New spines tend to be darker than old ones. As the plants enter dormancy, these signs disappear. When growing, succulents need as much light as possible, short of burning; during their rest period, much less.

Professional nurserymen often cultivate succulents and cacti in lathe houses or greenhouses, where the plants receive bright light but no direct sun. Such plants, when brought home, may need to be hardened off (gradually introduced to greater light) lest they sunburn. Should tissues become scorched, the succulents likely will survive, but their appearance may be spoiled by unsightly brown or beige patches. I tent new plants with window screens left in place one hour less each successive day.

Very few succulents thrive in full shade. Exceptions include haworthias and sansevierias—but even those do best when given these ideal conditions for all succulents: several hours of early morning and/or late afternoon sun, and filtered sun or bright shade during the hottest part of the day.

WINDOWSILL GARDENS

The direction your windows face plays a role in how well your windowsill succulents will do. In the Northern Hemisphere, south-facing is the sunniest, followed by east-facing, then west, then north. Light magnified by window glass may burn your plants; protect them from harsh sunlight by moving them farther from the glass and/or adding a sheer curtain.

Light intensity also varies according to how high your windows are; those on your home's top story will receive more light than those downstairs. The time of year is a factor as well. Deciduous vines and trees that shade windows in summer are without leaves in winter, letting in more light. But winter's dim light may be insufficient for sun-loving succulents. If this is the case, provide supplemental light, lest plants etiolate (stretch toward a light source). Rotate your windowsill plants occasionally so their growth is not lopsided. And when temperatures drop, make sure the plants are not too close to cold glass.

(top) Three pots aligned on a windowsill hold *Opuntia microdasys* 'Monstrosus', *Parodia haselbergii*, and haworthias. Chicweed (pot on far right).

(middle) The winter landscape outside the window has snow and bare branches, but inside, windowsill succulents (notably a rebutia cluster, *Pachypodium namaquanum*, and *Ferocactus glaucescens*) are unfazed. A metal-mesh shelf beneath the plants enhances air circulation. Sylvia Lin residence, Ambler, PA. Photo by Rob Cardillo.

(bottom) A teapot-sized strawberry jar on a kitchen counter holds sedum and sempervivum rosettes. Barbara Baker residence, Rancho Santa Fe, CA.

POTTING AND REPOTTING

Although cacti and succulents can be planted or repotted anytime, when they are emerging from dormancy is ideal—fresh soil and a roomier container ensure optimal growth. This is especially true for those that are pot-bound (have filled their pots with roots, resulting in a diminished ability to absorb water and nutrients). Potting up is moving plants that have grown too big for their containers into larger ones.

If you are fastidious, clean previously used pots inside and out; if not, merely clean the outside (unless you are battling a pest infestation; then the inside will need scrubbing as well). Before filling a pot with soil, cover the drain hole with a piece of plastic or fiberglass screen so the soil does not wash out. You also can cover the hole with a piece of paper towel; by the time the paper disintegrates, roots will have knit together above the hole.

A countertop or table makes potting and repotting plants much easier than trying to work with objects lower than waist height, on a bench or on the floor. Spread a tarp, plastic drop cloth, or newspapers to protect your work surface (and to make cleanup easier), then slide the plant out of its pot. If it does not come out easily, do not pull on it—doing so may cause it to break at the crown (where stem and roots meet). Instead, invert the container and, while cradling the plant, tap the pot rim on the table edge. Or if the plant is in a plastic nursery pot, squeeze it to loosen the soil.

Check to see if roots are healthy and free of root mealybugs, slugs, sowbugs, and other pests. Untangle and prune roots growing in circles or that have become compacted. If you are refreshing a pot that held several plants, wiggle apart roots of those you want to save and discard the rest. Behead the gangly, long-stemmed rosettes of echeverias and aeoniums, and take cuttings from trailers such as senecios and graptopetalums. Avoid transplanting roots of weeds or their seeds along with your prized plants. This can be difficult when the weed has underground corms, like oxalis does. Unthread its leaves, stems, and roots from those of other plants—unfortunately, not an easy job, especially if oxalis is growing among barbed or spiky succulents—and discard, along with contaminated soil.

Avoid touching glochids (thin spines that radiate from cactus areoles). Wear gloves and hold the spiny plant with kitchen tongs or forceps, or wrap it in crumpled newspaper or a rolled-up towel. If glochids do become embedded in your skin, paint the affected area with rubber cement; let it dry, peel it off, and the glochids should go with it.

Fill the new pot half full of fresh soil, then position the succulent in the middle of the pot with its roots spread out. Add more soil—pressing it with your hands to anchor the plant—until the crown is about an inch below the rim (to leave room for water). Do not skimp on soil; a plant that sits too low in its pot will appear to be hiding. On the other hand, do not position the plant so high that it looks like it is going to fall out. Water thoroughly to settle the soil, then add topdressing.

Although columnar and tree succulents need deep pots, most succulents tend to be shallow rooted, so soil in the lower half of tall containers goes to waste. To save soil and reduce the pot's weight, fill the bottom half with plastic bags stuffed with packing peanuts (use those made of Styrofoam, not biodegradable cornstarch). Place permeable landscape cloth over the bags so that water will drain but soil cannot fall through. Then fill the rest of the pot with soil. It is also possible to pour packing peanuts into the bottom of the pot and soil on top, but soil mixed with Styrofoam creates a mess difficult to dispose of later on. A deep pot with no ballast may be top heavy—so I do not recommend this method for pots that will contain tall plants, especially in windy areas.

Some succulents are not worth repotting because they are so easily replaced—supermarket kalanchoes (*Kalanchoe blossfeldiana*) come to mind. These plants, after blooming in waves for a year, become disheveled. They are readily available, so I consider them annuals. But I do take cuttings if the color of the flowers is unusual and I want more.

Confinement slows the growth of potentially large succulents—which will stay smaller for longer than their twins growing in the open garden—but eventually potting up or root pruning is necessary. Show-quality succulents are routinely root-pruned to bonsai them and to prevent expanding roots from cracking the container. Those of fast-growing ficus may need pruning every year; slow-growing cacti, every four to six.

Small succulents such as haworthias and lithops may contentedly occupy the same pot for a decade or more. Noted succulent expert Myron Kimnach, a longtime collector of lithops and conophytums, advises people to move every ten years because "upheaval is good for you"—to which he adds, "And don't repot your conophytums more often than you move."

SOIL AND FERTILIZER

Succulents do best in a well-aerated potting mix that allows water to penetrate easily and drain rapidly, and that is not prone to compaction. Evaluate a potting soil's suitability by taking a handful and squeezing tightly; if it holds together when you open your palm, it needs amending.

Avoid using garden soil in your containers, because it harbors pests and may drain poorly. Also, many soilless potting mixes sold at nurseries are not recommended for cacti and succulents, because of a high percentage of peat. (Read the ingredients on the label.) Peat efficiently retains moisture, but when bone dry it shrinks and repels water. If this happens, the pot will need to be submerged to be rehydrated; you may have to hold it underwater because the block of soil will float.

It is possible to buy bagged "cactus mix," but for less money you can make your own. Amend any quality potting medium so that your final mix consists of one-third to one-half crushed volcanic rock (pumice), coarse-grained sand, and/or perlite (sometimes called sponge rock)—a ratio that can vary widely with no detriment to the plants. Coarse-grained sand is sometimes referred to as sharp sand because it feels sharp when rubbed between thumb and forefinger. Poultry grit, available at farm supply stores, also works well, as does builder's sand from home improvement stores. Do not use beach sand, which is salty and so fine it compacts—as does playground sand.

An economical way to obtain crushed volcanic rock in quantity is to purchase it at tack and feed stores; one brand is Dry Stall. Some growers prefer calcined clay (such as Turface, a product designed to enhance drainage on baseball fields); it consists of lightweight particles honeycombed with air pockets.

Depending on your area and the minerals in the water, salts may build up in the soil, which can cause succulents to yellow and grow sluggishly or not at all, and which may lower their resistance to pests and diseases. To flush soil of accumulated salts, water thoroughly each time (until it flows out the bottom of the pot).

When you water, you are not only leaching harmful salts and hard-water minerals from the soil, you are also removing, to some extent, beneficial salts and minerals. To counteract this, when planting or repotting add 1 tablespoon of slow-release granular fertilizer per gallon of soil mix. At the beginning of each subsequent growing season (which for most succulents is spring), apply an all-purpose, low-nitrogen (N number less than 12) liquid

POTTING MIXES: WHAT THE EXPERTS USE

It seems every succulent collector or nursery owner has a preferred potting mix. Some examples:

❋ A former CSSA president in New Jersey combines three parts commercial potting mix that is high in bark or horticultural coir with two parts pumice and one part calcined clay.

❋ A specialist in succulent bonsai recommends a mix of one part compost, one part coir, one part loam, and four parts pumice or perlite.

❋ A designer of succulent topiaries and wreaths uses no soil but rather inserts cuttings into tightly packed sphagnum moss.

❋ A kalanchoe collector's preferred mix is 50 percent pumice, 25 percent loam, and 25 percent decomposed granite sand.

❋ A haworthia grower mixes equal parts grit or plaster sand, pumice, and peat-free commercial potting soil.

❋ A collector who owns a wide range of succulents says it does not matter what base is used, so long as one-third to one-half of the final mix is pumice.

❋ An article in the CSSA newsletter recommends that at least half the mix consist of "an air-trapping substance" such as perlite, pumice, or calcined clay.

❋ A lithops collector's mix is "more white than brown": one-third commercial potting soil with twigs removed, and two-thirds perlite or pumice. He also may add decomposed granite "to help toughen the plants."

❋ A nursery owner who sells at shows prefers an easy-to-rewet mix of half-and-half coir and perlite.

❋ A cactus and succulent nursery in New Mexico recommends three parts soilless potting mix, one part coarse sand, and one part volcanic scoria, perlite, crushed gravel, or crushed limestone.

❋ A designer at a Denver nursery mixes half-and-half potting soil and poultry grit (crushed granite).

❋ A cactus and succulent show judge, emphasizing the importance of oxygen for roots, recommends not adding vermiculite, because it compacts.

Pumice.

fertilizer diluted to half strength. Or—especially if you are growing succulents in quantity for the commercial marketplace and need uniformly perfect plants—apply liquid fertilizer diluted to one-quarter strength, every four to six weeks during active growth. Never fertilize a dry plant; moisten the soil first.

Cacti and succulents prefer slightly acidic soil; the ideal pH is between 5.6 and 6.0. (A pH of 7.0 is neutral; below 7 is acidic, above 7 is alkaline.) Irrigating with tap water may tip the balance toward alkalinity, and roots will not be able to efficiently access nutrients. To test this, add 1 tablespoon (no more, or roots may burn) white vinegar per every 5 gallons of tap water. Observe the results after your plants have received this for a month or two. You may notice a remarkable increase in vitality as roots take up unlocked nutrients. Plants will have used the residue after the first few applications of acidulated water, so at that point begin fertilizing.

No feeding is necessary if no growth is desired, which is the case when succulents are used in wreaths, topiaries, floral-style arrangements, bonsai, and miniature landscapes. Also take care not to overfertilize; too much nitrogen can cause softening of tissues and make the plants susceptible to rot (cacti are particularly at risk).

WATERING: How Much and When

If you are a newcomer to succulents but are adept at gardening in containers, you may find it difficult to refrain from watering succulents as much as your other plants. After all, many common houseplants—such as ferns—may suffer if not drenched several times weekly. But the larger the succulent and the fatter its leaves, the longer it can, and should, go without water.

Although a good rule for watering cacti and succulents is "when in doubt, don't," keep in mind that roots that go bone dry will die. Root hairs—the plants' delicate water-absorbing filaments—need some moisture to stay viable. During periods of drought, succulents will live off their own well-sealed leaves, but for the plumpest and healthiest plants—especially during active growth—keep soil about as moist as a wrung-out sponge.

Many succulents will indicate by their appearance if they need water; learn to read the plant for telltale signs such as shriveling, and leaves that lose their sheen. If soil has pulled away from the inside of the pot or a chopstick inserted into the soil comes out dry (or nearly so), it is time to water. Do not use softened water, which contains salts and calcium.

Actively growing succulents should be watered anywhere from once a week to once a month, depending on the type of plant, the size of the container (larger pots hold more soil and therefore retain more moisture), the type of pot, and the weather. Potted succulents growing in high humidity do not need watering as often as those in low humidity, because arid conditions wick moisture away. Plants in containers that dry out quickly, such as unglazed clay pots or moss-lined baskets, need watering more often than those potted in a nonporous material, such as plastic. Tropical and rain forest succulents (such as schlumbergera and rhipsalis) like consistently moist soil; desert succulents, especially cacti, prefer to go dry (or nearly so) between waterings.

Gradually reduce the amount of water your succulents receive as their growth slows and their dormant period approaches, unless you will be keeping the plants at temperatures of 60 degrees F or higher; the warmer they are, the more water they will need. If your succulents are outdoors during their winter dormancy and your area experiences a week or two of unseasonably warm weather, water them lightly to keep their delicate root filaments viable.

The colder the plants, the less water they need. Moreover, succulents generally considered frost tender will fare better during a brief freeze if kept dry than if their tissues are engorged. Some growers insist that chilled and dormant succulents need no water at all; others give small amounts to prevent roots from desiccating. The latter practice helps to keep rotund cacti such as gymnocalycium plump and therefore less likely to split their skins when they awaken in spring and take up water to fuel growth.

When watering dormant succulents and cacti, pour water onto the soil (not onto the plants), aiming to keep it barely moist. Gradually increase the quantity and frequency as plants emerge from dormancy. Most cacti and succulents do not like being both damp and cold, so water in the morning to ensure that plants will dry by evening, when temperatures drop. Room-temperature water is best; water that it is too cold—especially if plants are unused to it—will stress them.

Rainwater is acidic and therefore excellent for potted succulents. Move your container gardens where they occasionally will be bathed by rain, or collect it in buckets and use it when watering. Most succulents are efficient at funneling water to their roots—a fact that becomes evident when you notice how the leaves of rosette succulents are arranged in a downward whorl, and

These succulent cuttings grow in a pot in Hilo, Hawaii, that is so constantly moist due to rainfall, it is coated with moss. The potting medium is porous, lightweight, crushed lava rock.

how the ridges of cacti and the foliage of agaves are concave, like rain gutters. But avoid pouring water onto cacti covered with white filaments—it makes them stringy—and succulents with a chalky or powdery coating (such as dudleyas and some cotyledons).

Not all succulents dislike a lot of water. It is not unusual to see cold-climate succulents such as sedums and sempervivums in containers that receive so much rain the surface of the pot is moss encrusted. Even dry-climate succulents will likely survive if their roots can breathe—especially if the weather is warm and the plants are not dormant. The most dramatic example I have seen of dry-climate succulents enduring far more water than they needed was in Hilo, Hawaii, a city that receives in excess of 100 inches of rainfall a year. There, *Agave attenuata* grows in gardens, and smaller succulents—notably jade, graptopetalums, and kalanchoes—thrive despite having their roots continually bathed by warm water.

If you live in an arid region where rainfall is sparse or nonexistent for months on end, acquire the habit of recycling clean water that otherwise would go down the drain. Before I discard a partially full bottle of drinking water, for example, I empty its contents onto my potted plants.

To conserve water and protect your garden (potted and otherwise) from getting too much, your automatic irrigation system should have a rain sensor that overrides it and shuts it off when necessary. Revise the schedule according to the plants' seasonal requirements. For example, in October, in anticipation of my garden's impending dormancy and cooler, wetter weather, I reprogram my automatic system to reduce the frequency and quantity of irrigation. In November or December, I turn the system off; in March or April, back on.

A convenient, efficient way to water potted succulents is with drip tubing, but it can look messy if not concealed, especially when a tube extends from the ground to the top of a tall pot. To water such a pot without tubes showing, prior to planting, extend tubing up through the hole in the bottom, all the way to the rim. Then add a T adapter to make the tube branch, with an emitter on each end.

The shape of a pot makes a difference when it comes to water retention. Succulents like to spread their roots laterally, which is one reason they typically are grown in wide, shallow pots—which also offer even distribution of moisture. Cylindrical pots have drier soil near the top and a reservoir of moist soil at the bottom. Although this better serves ornamental plants with long taproots, it does succulents no harm.

If a composition has a decorative topdressing, take care not to dislodge it; use a turkey baster or a watering can with a long, slender spout to gently apply water to the base of the plant. This will also prevent water spots (which are caused by dissolved minerals) from forming on leaves.

Rot is not immediately apparent because it first damages roots; you likely will not know anything is amiss until the plant's trunk or stem is mushy. Overwatered cacti and succulents that have succumbed to rot may be salvageable. Using a sharp knife, excise any soft tissue, making sure to get every bit. Sterilize the blade (wipe with rubbing alcohol) and make the final cut through firm, healthy tissue. Allow this to heal, then root the salvaged plant as you would any cutting, in fresh soil.

Watering containers that lack drainage

Now that you have the rules for watering potted succulents, bear with me and set them aside.

Consider: if you carefully limit the amount of water your potted succulents receive to only the amount they need to survive, it is possible—and even desirable in light of the creative opportunities—to grow succulents in containers that have *no* drainage. In other words, if you merely and only occasionally dampen the growing medium (using filtered water free of salts), you can cultivate succulents in a sugar bowl.

POT FEET, PADS, AND WHEELS

It is important to elevate pots so that air can circulate beneath them, and ants, slugs, and sowbugs cannot enter via drain holes. Raising containers even slightly helps protect flooring from water stains and moisture damage, and prevents indelible rings from forming on hardscape.

Pot feet resemble doorstops but have a ledge for the bottom of the pot to sit on, and a knob or bump to keep it from sliding off. Terracotta is the material most commonly used, but ornamental feet of glazed clay and even glass are available. A pot needs three feet to support it securely.

Two-inch-diameter plastic half-spheres (one brand is Pot Pads) are a less-expensive alternative. Each upside-down dome—which has a flat rubber side that hugs the bottom of the pot—comes into minimal contact with the floor. The discs allow half an inch of air space beneath pots, are unobtrusive, and make it possible to slide the pot short distances.

Saucers on casters elevate pots and make heavy ones easy to move. But unless you live in a dry, hot climate, water that collects in the saucers may not evaporate quickly and will need to be blotted lest roots rot.

Glazed ceramic pot feet match the container, which is planted with a red bromeliad, red-flowering *Euphorbia milii*, red-stemmed *Portulacaria afra* 'Variegata' *Sedum nussbaumerianum*, and cascading *Lepismium cruciforme*. Kathryn O'Bryan garden, San Diego, CA. Design by Michael Buckner.

Pot feet of terracotta.

(right) Pots atop saucers on casters hold silver dollar jade (*Crassula arborescens*) in bloom. Scott Glenn garden, Santa Barbara, CA.

CHICWEED'S TECHNIQUE FOR POTTING IN NONDRAINING CONTAINERS

Susan and Melissa Teisl and Leah Winetz of Chicweed, a florist shop and garden boutique in Solana Beach, California, routinely plant succulents in antique bowls, wood drawers, soufflé dishes, and other appealing vessels that lack drain holes. If the container is a porous material, such as wood, they line it with plastic to protect it from soil and moisture. Next comes a layer of gravel, then potting mix to 2 inches below the rim. After they plant the container with an assortment of succulents from 2-inch pots, they trim the plastic and using a chopstick, tuck the remaining inch or so under to conceal it. They brush dirt particles from the plants' leaves, then water the arrangement lightly to settle the soil. Under normal conditions, the plants need no additional water for several weeks.

To prepare an antique oak drawer for planting, Melissa Teisl lines it with black plastic secured with blue masking tape, then adds a layer of gravel. Chicweed, Solana Beach, CA.

The designer arranges succulents (rhipsalis and echeverias) in the drawer, much as she would a floral arrangement.

The next step is to trim the plastic and tuck it into the container, where it will not show. Flat pebbles will conceal any gaps.

A soft paintbrush removes dirt spilled onto the leaves.

The final step is to water lightly to settle the soil, but not so much that the water puddles.

This may seem counterintuitive, considering how easily the roots of succulents rot. But it makes sense when you realize how little water plump plants need. The problem arises when the owner's urge to water kicks in. For example, I was given a floral-style arrangement of haworthias that have fat, turgid leaves, in a coffee-mug-sized pot with no drain hole. I dribbled pure, filtered water into the arrangement—about an ounce at a time—on average once every three weeks. (And many more times than that, I persuaded myself not to.) After six months, the haworthias, except for enlarging slightly, looked the same as originally. But several lovely little cryptanthus bromeliads, each the size of a dime and forming a bowlike cluster, had given up the ghost.

Some designers place a layer of aquarium charcoal in the bottom of a container that lacks drainage, to act as an absorbent and to aid in keeping the soil sweet. Others add a layer of pumice, crushed lava rock, or gravel. I am not convinced any of these make a difference; my preference is simply to use a fluffy soil mix.

Bear in mind that succulents grown in containers without drainage normally are not there for the long term. Such compositions should be regarded as floral arrangements with staying power. Do not leave any container that lacks drainage out in the rain, nor situate it where it will be overwatered by automatic irrigation.

GROOMING

Just as weeding and tending garden beds can be relaxing, so can grooming and tidying your potted succulents. I keep tools in a small bucket handy for toting from plant to plant. Others bring the pots to the tools, in a greenhouse, shed, or designated garden work area.

Tools you might find useful include a soft toothbrush or small paintbrush for cleaning fuzzy leaves, a flathead screwdriver for detaching pups from agaves, a plastic spoon for adding fresh topdressing, soft bonsai wire for training limbs, a steak knife for slicing through fibrous tissue, and a chopstick for determining soil moisture or nudging gravel into place. Kitchen shears or clippers with long handles and narrow blades are good for trimming hard-to-reach branches, dried leaves, and spent blooms. When a thumb and forefinger are too clumsy for tasks such as removing a pine needle from cactus spines, I use long-handled tweezers. Hemostats, which resemble scissors but are specialized for gripping, can clamp onto the base of a weed or a bit of debris and hold it securely while it is extracted. And kitchen tongs make it easy to grasp small cacti while transplanting them.

Wearing gloves is a good idea whenever gardening. I keep handy a box of disposables, should I want to keep dirt from getting under my fingernails or to protect my hands when I take cuttings from euphorbias, which have sticky, caustic sap. My all-purpose gardening gloves are flexible calfskin, which is adequate for all but the prickliest plants. Growers of large cacti and agaves recommend welders' gloves.

If a succulent naturally has a powdery coating, use your breath to dislodge any dirt particles, because brushing or otherwise touching the leaves will cause the powder to rub off. A well-directed spray of water is also a good way to clean plants, providing it does not scatter topdressing and soil. If smooth-leaved succulents look dull because of water spots, remove them with a soft cloth moistened with distilled water. Cacti covered with long white filaments can be gently brushed and even—according to a CSSA judge—shampooed.

Make sure drain holes are not plugged or caked with dirt, which often is the case when containers sit on garden soil. Check for pests and spray as needed, and decide whether new growth needs trimming or thinning. Have an empty nursery flat or tray ready to receive pups and cuttings, which then can be used to make new arrangements.

OVERWINTERING

The arrival of winter and impending freezing temperatures (32 degrees F and lower) means that frost-tender succulents—which are the majority—should be brought indoors or otherwise protected. If your succulents are not valuable or difficult to replace, one option is to leave them to their fate. Those that make it through the winter, consider perennials; the rest, annuals.

If you live where freezing temperatures are occasional and brief, covering your succulents may be all that is needed. On those nights when frost is predicted, drape the plants with a sheet—taking care that the spines of agaves and cacti do not become embedded in the fabric—and then remove it the next morning. Know your garden's microclimates; plants on a patio will benefit from warmth radiated by walls and eaves. Those in the garden, out in the open, are more vulnerable.

Frost-damaged leaves darken, then soften, and in a day or so turn putty-colored. Remove the damaged leaves lest they invite rot into the crown, then shelter the plant until all danger of frost has passed. If frost has burned the ends of the leaves only—often the case with aloes—do not prune until spring, as tips protect healthy tissue lower down. For aesthetic reasons, rather than cutting straight across, follow the shape of the leaf.

Succulents that survive temperatures well below freezing include orostachys and jovibarbas; most sempervivums, sedums, and yuccas; and some cacti and agaves. But even frost-hardy succulents do not like prolonged rainy weather and will need protection from excess moisture—which may be as simple as moving them beneath your home's eaves.

When estimating the cold hardiness of a succulent you are considering overwintering outdoors, keep in mind that a plant in a container is more vulnerable to cold than one growing in the ground, because greater soil mass acts as an insulator. For example, an opuntia that is hardy to zone 6 will experience conditions, when in a pot, better defined as zone 5. But even if a plant can withstand freezing temperatures, its container—if made of porous clay—may not.

When you bring your container-grown succulents indoors for the winter, group them as much as possible according to their native habitats, with the goal of providing similar seasonal temperatures, light, air circulation, and humidity.

Your basement is likely the best location to overwinter cacti and other desert succulents; areas of your home that are comfortable for you will be too warm for these plants—which should be kept at 55 degrees F or lower. Even temperatures close to freezing will not harm them, if introduced gradually. Desert temperatures in midwinter drop at night to 40 degrees F or below, and daytime highs may not exceed 60 degrees F. Cold not only is part of the plants' natural cycle, it also triggers dormancy, which is essential for flowering.

Dormancy does not mean darkness. Provide the light that cacti and succulents need with 40-watt bulbs on timers programmed to stay on for 10 to 12 hours daily. Use fluorescent bulbs; they are inexpensive, and quiescent plants do not need a broad-spectrum light source. To discourage pest infestations, keep a fan running to circulate air.

Summer-dormant winter growers, such as aeoniums and senecios, should be overwintered in your home's warmer areas. These succulents need a minimum of six hours of bright light daily, or they will etiolate.

If your winters are not severe but temperatures dip below freezing for extended periods, you may want to avoid the daily bother of draping your frost-tender succulents and instead shelter them within cold frames—long, low structures lined with panels of translucent polycarbonate. Or install a minigreenhouse that extends outward from an exterior wall of your house; such a lean-to benefits from your home's warmth, and by being close to electrical outlets, makes it fairly easy to add a heater or fan. A downside to lean-to greenhouses, however, is that they may not get enough sunlight.

A freestanding greenhouse is the best option if you have the budget and space. Such a structure allows you to control the amounts of light, ventilation, heat, and humidity your potted succulents receive. The greenhouse, which ideally has doors that open wide enough for a wheelbarrow, should be within easy access of your home and near a hose bib. Locate it in a level area

This shallow pot and the sedums and sempervivums it contains remain outdoors during the Massachusetts winter. In spring, the owner freshens it by replacing plants as needed and fills gaps with decorative stones. Fran and Clint Levin garden, Dartmouth, MA. Photo by Charles Mann.

This greenhouse was custom built by Gary Mallen to house his wife's assortment of cacti and succulents in collectible pots. Uncluttered shelves arranged like bleachers enhance air circulation and enable plants and pots to be seen easily. Collection of Wanda Mallen, Fallbrook, CA.

of your yard that gets at least six hours of sun daily in winter. To maximize winter sun, and for even, all-day exposure, align cold frames or a greenhouse with the sun's east-west path.

Every region has its own challenges. If you are uncertain how to overwinter your cacti and succulents, and before investing in a greenhouse, consult members of the closest Cactus and Succulent Society of America chapter and ask for recommendations. Founded in 1929 in Pasadena, California, the CSSA has more than 80 affiliated clubs and thousands of members worldwide.

For example, a collector near San Antonio installed a greenhouse to get his plants through winter temperatures in the low 20s F. He was pleased with the structure in winter and hoped to keep plants in it year-round. But in summer, its lone roof vent proved inadequate. Even with the double doors propped open and a good breeze, temperatures within the greenhouse exceeded 120 degrees F. He now drapes the structure with shade cloth in summer and advises anyone considering the purchase of a greenhouse—especially in south Texas—to make sure it can be vented adequately.

When returning potted succulents from their winter shelter to your patio or garden, take care that the plants do not sunburn. Those in a greenhouse may also need protection when months of overcast skies give way to bright sunshine.

PESTS AND DISEASES

Insects that cause container-grown succulents the greatest problems are mealybugs, aphids, scale, spider mites, and thrips—all of which feed on tender new growth, buds, and newly opened blooms. Plants grown in close quarters indoors are the most vulnerable; those outside that receive good air circulation and an occasional drenching seldom have problems.

Whenever you bring home a new plant, isolate it for a week, checking from time to time to see if it harbors pests. They spread rapidly, so if you find one, also check nearby plants. If an infestation gets out of hand, destroy affected plants by bagging them—complete with roots and soil—and putting them out with the trash. Clean containers thoroughly, as well as anything nearby in which the insects might shelter.

One telltale sign that sucking insects have colonized your plants is the presence of ants, which feed on the pests' sweet secretions. Treating the plant to get rid of the pests will usually rid it of ants as well. If ants have built a nest in the soil, the plant will need repotting.

Mealybugs appear to be bits of cotton, which the insect uses to house itself. Look for these in leaf axils (where leaves attach to the stem) and in the deep fissures of fat-leaved succulents such as lithops. Aphids and thrips are pinhead-sized oval beads that cluster along flower stems and buds. Spider mites look like particles of cayenne pepper, spin delicate webs, and reproduce rapidly on dusty plants—especially those in a dry, hot environment.

Infestations of mealybugs, aphids, thrips, and spider mites can be brought under control by hosing the plants with water or spraying them with insecticidal soap. I also keep a bottle of rubbing alcohol handy with a nozzle turned to a pinpoint spray, in order to target the bugs and desiccate them. I have not found alcohol to burn or otherwise damage leaves, but I also have not experimented on anything beyond echeverias, crassulas, and kalanchoes. If a cactus or succulent is valuable to you, test the spray on a small area and/or dilute it half-and-half with distilled water. Take care not to kill any beneficial insects (such as praying mantises, ladybugs, and lacewings) that feed on the bad ones.

Scale is not common on succulents, but when it does appear, it can be difficult to eradicate. Scale manifests itself as tiny (1/16-inch) oval brown dots on stems and leaves. A hard outer shell protects the bugs from insecticidal sprays, including alcohol, soap, and commercial pesticides. Safe inside its shell, the insect continues to consume plant tissue. Over time, leaves yellow and wither, and the infestation spreads. I summarily discard any scale-infested succulent, but if you have a prized specimen that you want to save, first isolate it from other plants. Then using your fingernail or a knife that is not sharp (to avoid damaging plant tissue), scrape off the scale. Wash the surface of the plant with warm water to which a mild detergent has been added, until clean and pest free. Keep the plant quarantined for several weeks, checking every so often to make sure the scale has not returned.

Root mealybugs are especially difficult to detect and eradicate. They live in the soil, where they latch onto roots and coat them with white tufts. A succulent can live for years with such an infestation, and you will be none the wiser until you notice it is not thriving. Because this is a pernicious pest that will move on to colonize other plants, discard affected plants and soil, and thoroughly clean containers. If you prefer to salvage the plants and it is not possible to propagate them from cuttings, wash the roots free of soil, then soak in a solution of insecticidal soap for several hours before potting afresh.

Cancerous growth on aloes is caused by a wind-borne, microscopic mite that readily spreads to other aloes, causing similar disfiguration. Excise all cancerous tissue, treat the aloe and any nearby with alcohol or insecticide, and isolate the plant from all other aloes for at least six months.

Snails and slugs may find their way into your containers from the garden; check the undersides of leaves as you groom your plants, and elevate pots so they do not sit on dirt or decaying leaves. Mildew may be a problem if your succulents stay damp; if moving them to a drier location does not help, apply horticultural fungicide.

NEW PLANTS FROM OLD

One of the great joys of cultivating succulents is that a single plant has the potential to provide many more. Cuttings root readily, and offsets (miniatures of the mother plant) are easily dug or wiggled loose and replanted.

Some designers routinely dip a cutting's raw end into rooting hormone. I have used this powder and also have rooted cuttings without it, and was not able to tell the difference. I confess, moreover, that I often do not wait for cuttings to callus before planting them. (A callus is a thin membrane that seals the cut end.) Although it makes sense to let juicy tissues heal before sticking them in soil teeming with microbes, I have observed even raw-edged and jagged cuttings take root and thrive. I should note that these were common, readily available succulents of minimal value. Obviously, the more important the cutting, the greater the care that should be taken to ensure its success.

When creating a composition comprised of fresh cuttings, water lightly at first to settle the soil and then not at all until roots have had a chance to form. Moist soil does encourage root formation, but there also is the danger that a cutting immersed in dirt and kept wet will rot.

Succulents are able to grow roots under remarkably adverse circumstances. In my garden *Agave americana* attests to this. I needed a plant to fill a gap quickly because I was hosting a garden event. The day before, I noticed a neighbor had put an *Agave americana* pup on the curb with the trash. The plant was about 18 inches in diameter and as tall. I brought it home and set it atop the ground in the gap. On the day of the event, no one knew that the agave was not really growing there, nor that it lacked roots. If someone had kicked it, it would have rolled down the slope. I considered removing it afterward, because I know how big such plants get, but since it was sitting on hard-packed decomposed granite I thought there was no danger of it rooting. So it stayed. That was spring, and by late summer, the tips of the leaves had shriveled. This was no surprise; temperatures were in the 90s, and the plant had no way to take up moisture—not that there was any moisture to be had. By fall, the agave looked significantly stressed, and I thought of removing it but did not get around to it. Winter rains came and went, and by spring, the agave had recovered. In four years, it tripled in size. In February, the bright yellow blooms of a nearby acacia contrast dramatically with the blue of the agave's leaves. In March, it is a sculptural focal point for a bank of purple-blooming drosanthemum. In April, satiny California poppies appear at the agave's base, their searing orange the perfect complement to the agave's blue. And when viewed from the house, the agave gives definition to that area of the garden. A friend who is a landscape designer advised me to remove the agave before it gets much bigger, because it will likely grow so large over the next few years that it will encroach on a pathway. I told him, when that happens I will move the pathway.

Perhaps initially I should have installed a large pot in the garden where the gap was, filled the container with potting soil, and set the agave pup atop it. Pup and pot would have served as an ornamental addition to the garden, and thus confined, the agave would have stayed small much longer—something I could have ensured by lifting it from the pot and pruning its roots.

Haworthia limifolia offsets.
Bob Kent garden, Poway, CA.

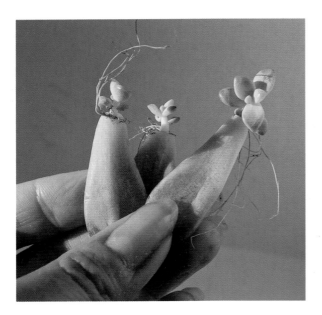

(top) Graptopetalum leaves show varying stages of plant and root formation.

(right) After the top half of this euphorbia was removed, new growth sprouted beneath the cut.

Eventually (in 10 or 15 years), my in-ground agave will complete its life cycle, requiring immediate and inconvenient removal to prevent an eyesore of significant proportions. Potting it would have enabled me to tame a behemoth now swelling ever larger and producing pups of its own.

All that is required for a succulent to root is viable growth tissue; in the case of my agave, this was the stem from which the leaves radiate. Some succulents need only a single leaf. If a succulent's plump leaves pop off easily (typical of graptopetalums, pachyverias, pachyphytums, and some sedums), it likely will produce new growth at the stem end. Lay a leaf atop slightly damp soil out of direct sunlight. Do not bury any part of the leaf, or keep it wet, lest it rot. Threadlike roots and tiny new leaves will form, feeding off the mother leaf and eventually draining it. As soon as their size warrants it, pot up the young plants.

Certain hybrid echeverias, such as fancy ruffled ones atop ever-lengthening stems, do not form offsets but are not difficult to propagate via beheading (removal of the rosette). Using a sharp knife, sever the head an inch or two below the lowest leaves. Set the echeveria rosette in an empty pot, in the shade, so its bottom leaves rest on the pot's brim. In a few weeks, roots will sprout from the cut end. Replant the head so its short stem is buried in coarse potting soil and its leaves are flush with the edge of the pot. Although only a headless trunk, keep the original potted plant. Give it bright light and regular water, and one or more rosettes will sprout from leaf axils. When these are larger than 2 inches in diameter, they can be cut from the stem and planted.

If you have a columnar cactus or euphorbia that has grown too tall, or a spherical cactus that has etiolated, hold it with tongs and slice through it horizontally at its midpoint or 6 to 10 inches below the top. Allow the cutting to callus, then pot it. The original plant will sprout new growth around the cut end, eventually hiding it and creating a crown of offsets. These can be left on the plant or removed and rooted.

Plantsman and show judge Tom Glavich, in the column he writes for the CSSA newsletter, shared suggestions for promoting rapid root growth in ceroid cuttings. Pot them first in pumice or (in the case of larger plants) gravel. Do not water but rather set the pot where ground moisture can seep through the bottom. Drawn toward moisture, roots will form quickly. After a few weeks, the cutting can be watered and after a few months (if roots are adequate) transplanted into a pot filled with a good cactus mix.

SEED PROPAGATION AND HYBRIDIZING

Many collectors enjoy propagating cacti and succulents from seed. I find seeds too fiddly and time consuming, and invariably, I forget to water seedlings or discover too late that the sun has broiled them. I do acknowledge, however, the rewards inherent in observing the range of variation in seed-grown plants, and in selecting offspring with pleasing forms and colors. Moreover, seeds are easily mailed to fellow enthusiasts who do not live nearby—indeed, may reside on different continents.

If you collect a particular genus, you have the potential to create intriguing crosses—hybrids that combine characteristics of their parents. Succulents that take readily to cross-pollination (thereby creating interspecific hybrids, meaning crosses of different species within the same genus) include aeoniums, aloes, echeverias, gasterias, graptopetalums, haworthias, lewisias, lithops, and most cacti.

Bob Kent of Poway, California, began collecting and hybridizing haworthias more than 30 years ago. The results now fill a dozen tables in an area of his garden sheltered by shade cloth, and fellow enthusiasts from as far away as Japan have come to visit. Kent's hybrids of *Haworthia magnifica* var. *major* and *Haworthia mirabilis* var. *badia* are shades of green, pink, and rose; those of *Haworthia truncata* have translucent leaf tips and veining that resembles starbursts and snowflakes.

Kent's suggestions for germinating and planting seeds and creating hybrids are based on his experience with haworthias but apply to other genera as well:

* When flowers open, use a clean artist's paintbrush to transfer pollen from one plant to another as though you were a hummingbird. To ensure fertilization, repeat this on several successive days. With haworthias, pollen transfer should be from the newest to the oldest flower.

* Watch for a seed capsule to form; this indicates that an embryo is developing within. When the dry capsule begins to split open, harvest the seeds. Those of haworthias resemble pepper flecks.

* Sprinkle 20 to 30 seeds atop moist potting soil (Kent prefers a mix of 60 percent pumice and 40 percent coir) in a 2- to 3-inch-diameter nursery pot. Cover seeds lightly with a thin layer of potting mix and gently spray with distilled water to which a slight amount of fungicide has been added.

* On a white plastic nursery tag or tongue depressor, record the names of the parents and the date you sowed the seeds. Keep that record with the offspring as they mature. You may also want to maintain a written log that corresponds to numbers you have assigned to batches of seed-grown plants.

Haworthia truncata hybrid in Bob Kent's collection.

✳ To ensure that the seedlings do not desiccate, put the pot in a clear plastic bag and seal it. Place the bag where it will receive adequate light and warmth: in a greenhouse; beneath two layers of shade cloth outdoors (in mild climates); under grow lights indoors (minimum of 16 hours a day); or on a windowsill that receives bright light but not direct sun. The ideal temperature range is 70 to 78 degrees F. Even soil in a sealed bag can dry out, so check the moisture occasionally.

✳ Remove the pot from the bag when seedlings are barley sized. Keep soil as moist as a wrung-out sponge.

✳ When seedlings begin to crowd each other, transplant them into a nursery tray with good drainage, filled with potting soil.

During the ensuing year or two, each hybrid will begin to reveal its unique characteristics. Pot up those plants you find most pleasing and discard the rest.

A fishing-tackle box planted with sempervivums, sedums, and graptopetalums incorporates the owners' shell collection. Design and photo by Mari Malcolm, Seattle, WA.

Succulents for Height

Use these as upright elements in larger compositions, to fill a blank wall or empty corner, and to provide eye-level interest. Some have the potential to get quite large when in the ground, but pot culture naturally dwarfs them.

adeniums
Aloe ferox
Aloe marlothii
Aloe plicatilis
beaucarneas
ceroids
cussonias
dasylirions
dracaenas
Euphorbia ammak
Euphorbia ingens
Euphorbia leucodendron

Euphorbia tirucalli 'Sticks on Fire'
Ficus palmeri
Kalanchoe beharensis
Myrtillocactus geometrizans
Operculicarya decaryi
pachypodiums
Portulacaria afra
sansevierias
synadeniums
uncarinas
yuccas

Midsized Succulents

Use these for mid-height interest in multiple-plant compositions and as all-purpose succulents in pots neither tiny nor large.

aeoniums
agaves (smaller species)
aloes (smaller species)
Bulbine frutescens
Cistanthe grandiflora
cotyledons
crassulas (jade type)
echeverias
Euphorbia milii
euphorbias, medusoid
Euphorbia trigona
gasterias
graptoverias
kalanchoes
lewisias
pachyphytums
sansevierias
sedums (shrub-forming)
senecios

Small Succulents

These work well in strawberry jars, miniature pots and landscapes, and as windowsill plants.

Aloe brevifolia
Aloe juvenna

Aloe 'Lizard Lips' and similar hybrids
Cotyledon tomentosa
crassulas
echeverias
Euphorbia obesa
Euphorbia suzannae
faucarias
haworthias
ice plants
living stones
mammillarias
parodias
rebutias
sedeverias
sedums
sempervivums
stapelias

Fillers and Cascaders

Use these in tall pots and hanging baskets, and to add over-the-edge interest to potted arrangements.

Aloe ciliaris
Aloe distans
Aloe juvenna
Ceropegia woodii
crassulas (stacked)
Disocactus flagelliformis
epiphyllums
graptopetalums
hoyas
ice plants

Lepismium cruciforme
Othonna capensis
portulaca
Portulacaria afra 'Variegata'
rhipsalis
sedums
sempervivums
Senecio herreanus
Senecio macroglossus
Senecio radicans
Senecio radicans 'Fish Hooks'
Senecio rowleyanus
Xerosicyos danguyi

Colorful Leaves

YELLOW

Crassula ovata 'Hummel's Sunset'
Echinocactus grusonii
Sedum 'Angelina'
Sedum makinoi 'Ogon'
Sedum nussbaumerianum

BLUE-GREEN

agaves
aloes
echeverias
Ruschia deltoides

BLUE

Agave 'Blue Glow'
Agave pumila
Aloe brevifolia
echeverias

Pilosocereus pachycladus (and other blue ceroids)
Sedum 'Blue Spruce'
Senecio mandraliscae
Senecio serpens

BLUE-GRAY

Agave marmorata
Agave parryi
Agave potatorum
echeverias
Sedum 'Blue Spruce'

PALE GRAY

Agave colorata
Agave gypsophila
Agave neomexicana

SILVERY GRAY

Agave montana
Crassula perfoliata var. *falcata*
cotyledons
dudleyas
Kalanchoe tomentosa
Sedum spathulifolium 'Cape Blanco'

RED AND RED-ORANGE

Aloe buhrii
Aloe cameronii
Aloe dorotheae
Aloe nobilis
Crassula 'Campfire'
Crassula pubescens

Crassula schmidtii
echeverias
Euphorbia tirucalli 'Sticks on Fire'
Gymnocalycium mihanovichii
Kalanchoe luciae
Sedum adolphi

ROSE, LAVENDER, OR PURPLE

Aeonium 'Garnet'
Crassula perforata
Echeveria 'Afterglow' or 'Perle von Nurnberg'
Graptoveria 'Fred Ives'
Kalanchoe pumila
Lepismium cruciforme
pachyphytums
Sempervivum 'Rojin'

MAGENTA-BLACK

Aeonium arboreum 'Zwartkop'
Echeveria affinis 'Black Knight' and 'Black Prince'

VARIEGATED WITH CREAM, WHITE, OR YELLOW

Aeonium 'Kiwi'
Aeonium 'Sunburst'
Agave americana 'Mediopicta Alba'
Agave americana 'Variegata'
Agave desmettiana 'Variegata'
Agave parryi 'Cream Spike'
Agave victoria-reginae

Agave victoria-reginae var. *ferdinandi-regis*
Aloe arborescens, variegated
Aloe nobilis
Aloe variegata and other partridge breast aloes
Crassula 'Calico Kitten'
Euphorbia ammak 'Variegata'
Euphorbia lactea 'Variegata'
Furcraea foetida var. *mediopicta*
Portulacaria afra 'Variegata'

VARIEGATED WITH RED OR PURPLE

Crassula perforata
Euphorbia trigona 'Rubra'
Kalanchoe marmorata
Mangave 'Macho Mocha'
Sempervivum 'Jungle Shadows' or 'Raspberry Ice'
Sempervivum tectorum
Senecio articulatus
synadeniums

Brilliant Flowers

aloes (yellow, orange, red)
Bulbine frutescens 'Hallmark' (yellow and orange)
cacti (white, cream, yellow, orange, red, magenta, purple, pink)
calandrinias (magenta-purple)
cotyledons (orange, salmon pink)

Crassula perfoliata var. *falcata*
(crimson)
Euphorbia milii (cream, yellow,
orange, red, pink)
ice plants (yellow, orange, red,
magenta, lavender, pink)
Kalanchoe blossfeldiana (white,
cream, yellow, orange, red,
magenta, pink)
lewisias (cream, yellow,
orange, rosy pink)

Textural Features

aloes
cacti
Cotyledon tomentosa
Crassula ovata 'Gollum' and
'Hobbit'
crassulas, stacked
crested succulents
dasylirions
dioscoreas
Echeveria pulvinata
echeverias, ruffled
Euphorbia milii
Euphorbia suzannae
gasterias
Kalanchoe beharensis
Kalanchoe tomentosa
sedums
sempervivums
Senecio rowleyanus
yuccas

Cold-hardy Cacti and Succulents

Plants are hardy to 20°F or to
lower temperatures if so indi-
cated.

Agave gentryi 'Jaws' (5°F)
Agave montana (−10°F)
Agave neomexicana (−20°F)
Agave parryi (−20°F)
Agave parryi subsp. *truncata*
(15°F)
Agave utahensis (−10°F)
Agave victoriae-reginae (15°F)
Agave victoriae-reginae var.
ferdinandi-regis (15°F)
Aloe polyphylla (10°F)
Aloe striatula (15°F)
Coryphantha vivipara (−20°F)
Crassula sarcocaulis (10°F)
delospermas (mountain
species)
Drosanthemum floribundum
Echinocereus coccineus (−20°F)
Echinocereus fendleri (−20°F)
Echinocereus polyacanthus
(−20°F)
Echinocereus reichenbachii
(−25°F)
Escobaria vivipara (−20°F)
Hesperaloe parviflora (−20°F)
jovibarbas
lewisias

Opuntia fragilis (−35°F)
Opuntia humifusa (−45°F)
Opuntia polyacantha (−25°F)
Opuntia trichophora (−30°F)
orostachys
sedums
sempervivums
yuccas

BIBLIOGRAPHY

Anderson, Edward F. 2001. *The Cactus Family*. Portland, OR: Timber Press.

Anderson, Miles. 2001. *A Gardener's Directory of Cacti and Succulents*. London: Anness.

Baldwin, Debra Lee. 2007. *Designing with Succulents*. Portland, OR: Timber Press.

Brenzel, Kathleen Norris, ed. 2007. *Sunset Western Garden Book*. Menlo Park, CA: Sunset Publishing.

Cave, Yvonne. 2002. *Succulents for the Contemporary Garden*. Portland, OR: Timber Press.

Colbert, Teddy. 1996. *The Living Wreath*. Layton, UT: Gibbs Smith.

de Vosjoli, Philippe, and Rudy Lime. 2007. *Bonsai Succulents*. Vista, CA: Advanced Visions.

Folsom, Debra Brown, ed. 1995. *Dry Climate Gardening with Succulents*. New York: Pantheon Books, Knopf.

Grantham, Keith, and Paul Klassen. 1999. *The Plantfinder's Guide to Cacti and Other Succulents*. Portland, OR: Timber Press.

Hobbs, Thomas. 1999. *Shocking Beauty*. Boston: Periplus Editions.

———. 2004. *The Jewel Box Garden*. Portland, OR: Timber Press.

Irish, Mary and Gary. 2000. *Agaves, Yuccas and Related Plants: A Gardener's Guide*. Portland, OR: Timber Press.

Kelaidis, Gwen Moore. 2008. *Hardy Succulents*. North Adams, MA: Storey Publishing.

Kramer, Jack. 1977. *Cacti and Other Succulents*. New York: Abrams.

Lyons, Gary. 2007. *Desert Plants*. San Marino, CA: Huntington Library Press.

Rogers, Ray. 2007. *Pots in the Garden*. Portland, OR: Timber Press.

Sajeva, Maurizio, and Mariangela Costanzo. 2000. *Succulents II: The New Illustrated Dictionary*. Portland, OR: Timber Press.

Smith, Gideon. 2006. *Cacti and Succulents*. Batavia, IL: Ball Publishing.

Smith, Gideon, and Ben-Erik van Wyk. 2008. *The Garden Succulents Primer*. Portland, OR: Timber Press.

Stephenson, Ray. 1994. *Sedum: Cultivated Stonecrops*. Portland, OR: Timber Press.

INDEX